CW00982939

a schizo-stroll:
anxious reflections on late capitalism

written by
a.t. kingsmith

with an afterword by
felix guattari*

a schizo-stroll:
anxious reflections on late capitalism
written by a.t. kingsmith
with an afterword by felix guattari*

*a previously untranslated paper of which
this text is in conversation with full permissions;
it serves this text both afterword and forwardly

designed by permanent sleep press
toronto, canada ©2017

ISBN-13: 978-1544802275
ISBN-10: 1544802277

direct all inquiries to:
https://adamkingsmith.com
akingsmith@protonmail.com

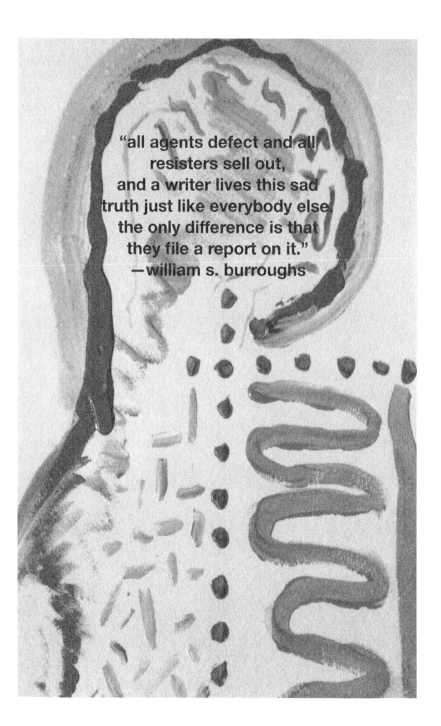

"all agents defect and all
resisters sell out,
and a writer lives this sad
truth just like everybody else.
the only difference is that
they file a report on it."
—william s. burroughs

introduction

part I. fractal ontologies

part II. schizoanalysis

part III. anxious capitalism

afterword/forward

notes

embarking on a schizo-stroll

"We must ask not what things 'do,' but how they 'work'." —Deleuze and Guattari

The proceeding schizo-stroll through the anxiety-inducing realities of late capitalism is a kind of homage to the revolutionary strategy put forward by Situationist Guy Debord in his 'Theory of the Dérive.'

The dérive is an experimental behaviour linked to the conditions of urban society: a technique of rapid passage through varied ambiances—an unplanned journey through a landscape, usually urban, in which participants attempt to drop their everyday relation and let themselves be drawn by the attractions of the terrain and the encounters they find there. They are necessary, I think, because of the increasingly predictable and monotonous experience of everyday life on the anxious terrain of late capitalism.

Though solo dérives are possible, Debord reminds us that the most fruitful way to explore any terrain is in a small group of two or three people who have reached a familiar awareness of the uncanny nature of modern society. That is exactly how this little book should be approached—with spirited cantor alongside friends as one strolls through the virtualised vistas and actualised wastelands of late capitalism. Studying the terrain of the city—a schizo-geography of affective alienation—one searches for visceral energies that can ignite the potential creation of revolutionary new Situations.

These rudimentary sketches are but a meandering attempt to help in that search. Of course, there's always a political motive behind any map—a motive that lives in the almost-invisible spaces between a map and the territory it seeks to represent. Like William S. Burroughs did with drugs, the motive here is to consider a very political problem: **"Can you harness the power of drugs without them taking over, without turning into a dazed zombie?"** It's the same with schizophrenia. 'I' make a distinction between schizophrenia as a process and the way schizophrenics are produced as clinical cases that need hospitalising—it's almost the same thing in reverse.

What connects schizoanalysts is an attempt to uproot from the social's causes and traditions in order to conduct physical exoduses from the ideological territories that have harboured us through much of our previous lives. In other words, to embark on a schizo-stroll is to embark on dérive of bodies, spaces, and times; of kinetics, materiality, and the non-conscious faces we present to the world. It is to strive for many heightened degrees of empathy and perception—to focus our gaze on something and tease out the intangible in it—an intangible that transforms something within each of us.

I'm not saying revolutionaries are schizophrenics. I'm saying there's a schizoid process, of decoding and deterritorialising, which only revolutionary activity can stop from turning into the production of capitalist paranoia. I'm considering a problem to do with the close

1

link between the reproduction of capitalism on the one hand, and between revolutionary movements on the other.

Schizoanalysts can talk in terms of capitalist anxiety and revolutionary schizophrenia because we're **not** setting out from a psychiatric-neoliberal understanding of these concepts, but rather from their social and political determinations—determinations from which their clinical application only follows in specific institutional circumstances.

It's not a question of being this or that sort of human, but of becoming inhuman, of a universal animal-becoming—not seeing human-beings merely as another animal, but unravelling our body's human organisation, exploring this or that zone of bodily intensity, with everybody discovering their own particular zones, and the groups, populations, and species that inhibit them. Becoming 'itself' has no fixed identity or being. It is always becoming-other. Alteration rather than alternation, pure difference rather than repetition, multiple becomings rather than a single, centralised, unitary standard of becoming.

Becomings have no history—a non-history constantly breaking out of the repressive inscription or encoding of the multiple lines within a unitary development. So who's to say 'I' can't talk about medicine unless I'm a doctor, if I talk about it like a fish? Who's to stop me talking about drugs without being an addict if 'I' talk about them like a bird? And why should't 'I' invent some way, however fantastic and contrived, of talking about something without someone having to ask whether I'm qualified to talk like that under the parameters of the vapid credentialism of the control society?

Like everything else, there are multiple ways to absorb the following schizoanalytical interventions: an academic way—which, in oscillating between condemnation and co-optation, either takes or leaves the texts in their integrity—and a revolutionary way—which takes and leaves them at the same time, doctoring them to its requirements in an attempt to use them to elucidate ones' own co-ordinates and guide ones' practices.

The only question is to try to make a text work. And, from this point of view, what has always been alive in revolutionary modes of thought, in their initial stages, is not the coherence of their statements, but the fact that the very act of enunciating them represents a breaking off, a way of telling the obsessive limitations of bourgeois political economy, academic psychology, the clinical psychiatry of the time, etc. to all go to hell.

In this spirit, schizoanalysis—and by extension, this precedent collection of schizo-strolls—has one single aim: *To get revolutionary, artistic, and performative machines working together as parts, cogs, of one another*.

After all, to embark on a schizo-stroll is to leave the furrow, to go 'off the rails,' to wander in imagination and thought—meanings, images, and so on float in a dream of dis-logic rather than calmly following from one to another along the familiar lines or tracks of cold reason. That's what these schizo-strolls are most interested in—a revolutionary schism necessitated by the current crises, the splitting off into post-capitalist worlds that, for now, only exists in those almost-invisible spaces between a map and the territory. Feel free to use them to fill in the blanks as 'you' see fit (and/or unfit),

—A.T., Toronto, Spring, 2017

2

part I. fractal ontologies

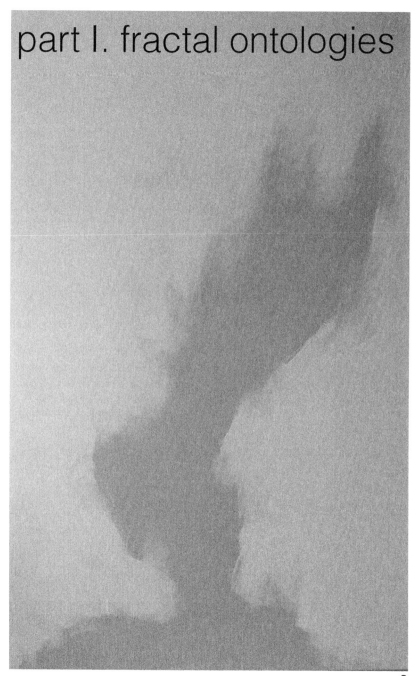

on reading with love

There are, you see, at least two ways of reading a work of philosophy.

You can see it as a box with something hidden inside and start looking for what it signifies, you can confine the text to an explicit meaning—a practice of crude and self- aggrandising reductionism. Then, if you're even more perverse and stubborn, you can treat the next work like another box contained in the first or containing it. And you can annotate and interpret and question, and write a book about the book, and so on and on.

You know the drill, it's all very rigorous. Maybe you even get rich.

Historicisation—fumbling, anxious, musty, unoriginal. Such indulgent misanthropies play a patiently repressive roll in the non-history of philosophy—it's philosophy's own version of the Oedipus complex: "You can't seriously consider saying what you yourself think until you've read this and that, and that on this, and this on that."

Or, there's this other way of reading. You see the work as a little non-signifying machine. Your only question is: "Does it work, and how does it work?" So how does it work for you? If it doesn't work, if nothing comes through, you try another book.

It's a strange process, thinking, reading for 'yourself,' because it doesn't at all come with seeing yourself as an ego or a person or a subject. We find a real name for ourselves, rather, only through the harshest exercise in depersonalisation—by opening ourselves up to the multiplicities everywhere within us, to the intensities running through us all.

A name born as the direct awareness of such intensive multiplicities is the opposite of depersonalization effected by this historicisation of philosophy —it's depersonalisation through creativity rather than subjection.

For what 'I' say comes from the depths of my ignorance, the depths of my own underdevelopment. 'I' become a set of liberated singularities, words, names, eyes, hairs, fingers, skin, things, animals, events—quite the reverse of a celebrity, 'I' melt.

Now listen here. This second way of reading, of thinking, it's intensive—something comes through, or it doesn't. There's nothing to explain, nothing to understand, nothing to interpret. You plug into an electric circuit. You are a computer.

There are people, 'I' know them. People who've never read a single work of philosophy who immediately see what a body without organs, a desiring-machine, or a plane of immanence are, given their own 'habits,' their own ways of experiencing these things, their own ways of becoming in the world.

As you can see, this second way of reading, thinking is quite different from the first because it relates a work directly to what's Outside.

A work—a work like this one—is a little cog in a much more complicated monastic machinery. Writing is but one flow among others—painting, dancing, singing, laughing, fucking. One flow with no special place in relation to the others.

Writing comes into fluid relations of currents and countercurrents, eddies and flows, more subjective flows—flows of words, flows of action, shit, sperm, money, technology, politics, anxiety, and so on and on.

Our outside, or at least one of our outsides, is a mass of people who are fed up with the ways in which capitalism diverts and syphons off these flows.

We're trapped because we generally continue in producing and reproducing capitalism at every level even after we've started to question the efficacy of its directives—to historicise, to demand of a work explicit meaning, something specific hidden within the box, is to read and to think on capital's terms.

But this more intensive way of reading, a perpetual depersonalisation in constant contact with what's outside the work, is a deterritorialising flow meeting other flows, one machine among others, as a series of experimentations for each reader in the midst of events that have nothing to do with writing.

To do this is to eat with your hands, to tear a book into pieces, getting it to interact with other things, absolutely anything—this is reading with love. And it is the only way to read and to think about philosophy as far removed from the terms dictated by capital as possible.

the problem of consciousness

what a world of unseen visions and heard silences,
this insubstantial county of the mind.

what ineffable essences,
these touchless rememberings and unshowable reveries,
and the privacy of it all.

a secret theatre of speechless monologues and prevalent council,
an invisible mansion of all moods, musings, and mysteries,
an infinite report of disappointments and discoveries.

a whole kingdom where each of us reigns:
recursively alone, questioning what we will,
commanding what we can,
a hidden hermitage where we may study out the book of what we
have done,
and yet may do.

an intro-cosm which is much more 'myself' than anything I can find in
a mirror.
this consciousness that is myself of selves,
that is everything,
and yet, it is nothing at all.

what is it?
where did it come from?
and why?

few questions have endured longer or traversed a more perplexing
history than this,
the problem of consciousness and its' place in nature.

despite centuries of pondering and experiment,
of trying to get together two supposed entities called mind and
matter in one age;
subject and object in another,

or soul and body in still others.

despite endless discoursing and experimentation,
ceaseless studies on the states or contents of consciousness,

despite distinguishing terms like intuitions, sense data, the 'given;'
the raw, feels, the sensa, presentations and representations,

despite recognising the sensations, images, and affectations
of poststructuralist and auto-ethnographical introspections,

despite the evidential data of scientific positivism,
the phenomenological fields, the apparitions of Hobbes,
the phenomena of Kant, the appearances of the idealist,
the elements of Nietzsche, the phantasm of Deleuze and Guattari…

…in spite of all of these,
the problem of consciousness is still with us,
something about it keeps returning,
not taking away a precedent solution.

on becoming-phenomenological

As 'I' come to an opening in this reflexive and meditative journey 'I' am alive with images and ideas, struck with the wonder of passionately discovering that the only way 'I' can truly come to know things and people is to go out to them, becoming-them, returning again and again to them, immersing myself completely in what is there before me.

Look, see, listen, hear, touch, dance, sing, laugh, shit, scream, fuck—from so many angles and perspectives and vantage points, each time freshly so that there will be continual openings and learnings that will connect with each other and with other prior perceptions, understandings, and future possibilities.

In other words, 'I' must immerse myself totally and completely in my world, take in what is offered without bias or prejudgment as much as possible. 'I' must pause and consider what my own life is and means, in conscious awareness, in thought, in reflections.

'I' enter into my own conscious reflections and meditations, open and extend my perceptions of life and reach deeper meanings and essences. This connectedness between what is out there, in its appearances and reality, and what is within me in reflective thought and awareness, is in truth, a wonderful gift of becoming. But knowledge does not end with moments of connectedness and meaning. Such journeys open vistas to new journeys for uncovering meaning, truth, and essence—journeys within journeys, within journeys.

This is perhaps the most telling reality of all, that each stopping place, every Being, is but a pause in arriving at knowledge. Satisfying as it is, it is but the inspiration for a new beginning, a becoming in perpetual continuance.

Knowledge as appearances and reasoned inquiry are not the end of knowing. No scientific discovery is ever complete. No experience is ever finished or exhausted. New and fresh meanings are forever in the world and in us. When the connection is made and the striving comes alive again, the process continues once more. There is no limit to our understanding or sense of fulfillment, no limit to our knowledge or experience of any concept, thing, or essence.

We need only to come to life again regarding some puzzlement and everything crystallizes in and through and beyond it. The whole process of becoming within something, becoming within ourselves, becoming within others, and correlating these outer and inner experiences and meanings is infinite, endless, imminent.

This is the beauty of knowledge and discovery, of A LIFE. It keeps us forever awake, alive, connected with what was, what is, and what will be—with what matters in life, with all imminent possible existences.

8

a radical happiness

A radical need not feel sad.

Sadness is a subtraction from our power—or rather, a seeming subtraction.

For our capacity to act remains the same, but our ability undergoes transitions and passages in la durée.

What sadness and hatred do—these reactive affections force us to divert some of our power, normally devoted to acting, back onto a trace or image of the thing hated.

The trace subtracts from our power to act. Depressed people are less able to act.

The trace of the hated thing is simply a dialectical opposition. Do we really need dialectical opposition to do politics?

We can be generous to those who suffer as long as it is not done out of pity—a reactive affection—but is done out of the overabundance of our power.

Eliminating the reactive traces and their dialectical oppositions is a way of getting back to this overabundance of power from which all becoming-revolutionary springs.

Of course, the assumption on the part of certain dialectical philosophers is that someone who is fulfilled and happy will not act to change the world. Such thinkers see negation as the only spur to action.

Yet tyrants need the people to feel sad so that they can maintain control. There is a term in schizoanalysis that depicts this—it is called 'anxiety.'

Put very simply, failure neurosis means that the person who wants success also fears it, so that any accomplishment is clouded by guilt.

This can be seen in the self-defeating thoughts of certain 'leftists': 'It is good that the right takes power because that will strengthen dialectical opposition.'

This statement expresses only self-pity, a reactive sense of disempowerment. We act more fully and more freely when we do not form oppositions.

We must stop making 'sense.' If we waste our power in self-defeating psychological games, we will never go out and radicalise our world.

So maybe the schizoids are right that radicals need not feel sad. We must think of a radical as happy.

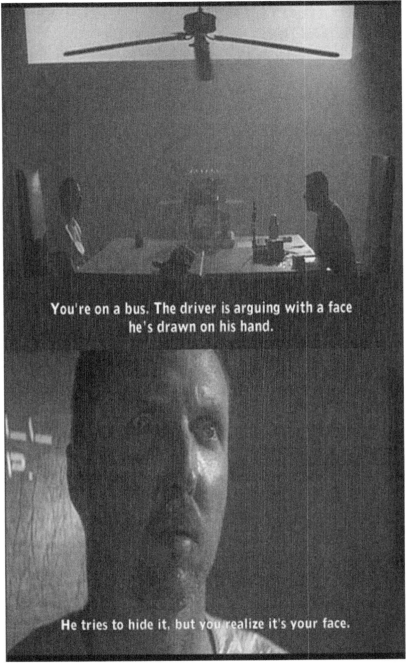

10

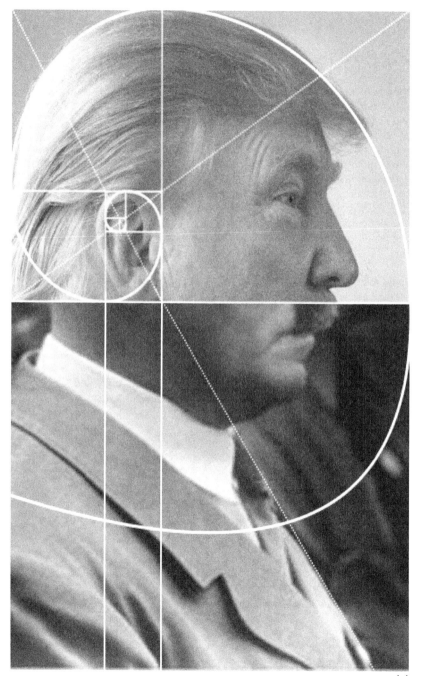

11

everything is networked, nothing is connected

the media has made such a mess of this age
and I read your poem
and I can tell it was another fantasy written on your iphone
because I can hear your binaric numbers and words
and I smell the static of electronic on your breath
and I can tell if a room is built in commercial computer-aided design
the second I walk in.

i feel these perfect round numbers,
these cookie-cutter walls and these ugly shitboxes
metastasizing the sprawl of the annex.
i feel the missing fractals in my cartilage.

and a mcmansion is a ouija board with meaningless signifiers
asking nothing, saying nothing.
and every mcmansion is built on an ancient burial ground
that stopped giving a shit fifty years ago
its sluggish spectres converted to slave labour capitalism.
they stopped haunting and got jobs at walmart.

but more progress, and more housing, and more skyscrapers and sprawl
developing in the gentrified cancer that invades the city
festering all the water
duplicating all the patterns
swallowing the illusory soul of cosmopolitanism.

with a flick of a commercial computer-aided design paintbrush
another flashy parking lot
another restaurant on some insignificant street
another piquant neighbourhood
another grilled cheese truck another sushi burrito.

copy and paste and paste and paste
and keep the maquiladoras pasting
and keep silicon valley metastisising
with really cool funky businesses
and really cool funky mcmansions
and really cool funky gentrified warehouse spaces
and really cool funky premium dive bars

12

this five dollar toast...is delicious.
omg is so good. you gotta fucking try it it's amazing.
4.2.

it's all so funky
it's all so cool
it's all so funkycool
the city is over
the city is proof of a coup.

the skins of the homeless are sewn into powerful slingshots
and they are used to deliver chewing gums and xbox games
to the programmers in their 40th floor apartment buildings.
the billionaires are evicting the millionaires.
their chariots run the children of the middle class down in the streets.
and still we beg for more
and i'm guilty too.

for there are viruses on the internet.
viruses to trap us all on our phones.
software that assures ibm builds better machine guns for the mind
a computers' childhood
as roko's basilisk.

open community and positivity!
california is dressed up in corporate venture capitalism
california is an app.
can we even blame capitalism any more?

it goes back to the spectacle itself
all those church councils
when we started separating ourselves from ourselves
separating minds from bodies
prying apart the unexpected convergences.

a phone is created
an app is invented
a connection is inserted into your connection
a cellphone, a line of code, an app, a cable, an uplink, a downvote.

mediation takes command, and we're all apps now.
and we click on each other amusing ourselves to death.
but thank god we're finally connected.
more and more connections!!
treating our data doubles like prized ponies.

13

making them race for karma.
we forget that we are forgetting
that reality is mediated through our phones
an invisible layer between us all
connecting us with extemporal transmitters.
they vibrate in our pockets and harvest our thoughts
harvest our visions, harvest our children, harvest the sky
the internet is feasting
the internet is the real world.

the compact disk is cliche the record is quaint
the vcr is novel
the cassette is trendy
the book has unexpectedly remained relevant in the north american market.

but the book is a computer
everything is a computer
three questions on six-times-two
digitalised desiring-machines.

we fed them the planet and in return the computers fed us our minds
in systemic prisons of endless mediation
a prison world of missed calls and text messages
a prison world of comprehensibly reconcilable emojis
a prison world of concepts that turn up ready-made.

and i can't see it
and you can't see it
and they can't see it
and we love to stay connected.

this prison is with us always
connecting us to the outside world
just inches above our eyes
as our heads stay down....
everything is networked but nothing is connected!!!

metamaterialist // manifesto

Metamaterials are materials engineered to have properties not yet found in the anthropocentric constitution of 'nature.' They are assemblages of conventional elements arranged in repeating—yet chaotic—patterns that derive properties not from their base materials, but from the precise size, shape, geometry, and orientation of their devised structures.

As such, metamaterial assemblages articulate a folding in of the arbitrary and anthropomorphic distinction between what is artificial and what is actual—a distinction Gilles Deleuze conceptualises re-articulates as the virtual and the real.

Such a folding is made visible through nonlinear dynamics—also known as chaos theory—a multidisciplinary field of study which has exposed the inherent structures underlying what were originally considered random forms and events in life. From the ultraviolet light of a computer and the formation of a mountain range to the fluctuations of the stock market and the reverberations of an electromagnet, everything exhibits deeply disordered 'structural' patterns.

It is these nonlinear patterns that give rise to the myriad shapes and events that we perceive to be real. No longer can material—virtual or real—taken to be an inert and lifeless substance that forces in the anthropocene act upon to create forms and patterns. Rather, materials have self-organisation, form, and pattern immanent to them —the epistemology of materiality as fundamentally anarchic.

To claim ontological differance between the material and the discursive is simply to repackage the dialectical trap of Cartesian dualism—the claim that in some respects, affective/discursive phenomena are non-material, or that affect and history aren't entirely co-constitutive. Metamaterialism ruptures this impasse by interpreting material and discursive aspects as abstractions from the same concrete encounter of event or phenomenological experience.

In speculating the ways that matter has some ontological and epistemological significance beyond that which humans consciously ascribe, metamaterialism adheres to a cosmologically distinctive and politically significant yet entirely fluid set of intertextual commitments:

I) The classic dualisms that constitute modernity—false binaries such as mind/ body, self/other, object/subject, theory/practice—are displaced by a non- reductive monism that emphasises the immanence of existence. Dialectical notions of matter as secondary to the forms imposed upon it are thus rendered obsolete by a molecular model in which vitality and activity are assumed to exist, and to have always existed, within energy-matter assemblages.

II) Futile attempts to transcend metaphysics in order to uncover the 'post-metaphysical' are overcome by a cosmological metaphysics of process that highlights the dynamic, temporal character of existence. Such metaphysics does not postulate a world where all being is in perpetual flux. Rather, it appreciates the differential nature of flows as a system moves through periods of relative equilibrium and periods of radical disequilibrium.

III) As the cosmos are composed of interacting forces with differing speeds and degrees of agency, metamaterialism requires a problem-orientation with all dimensions, from the microscopic to the planetary, folded in. In this way, a metamaterialist engagement is able to pursue the contours of a problem through tracing the interactive flows of strata at all levels of the continuum of existence—from the 'international' to 'individual'—as specific analyses require.

IV) Through experimentation, metamaterialism requires acting beyond the dictates of established knowledge in order to advance speculations about processes that currently exceed comprehension. To do so requires supplementing all present conceptions of reason and knowledge with radically experimental technologic-artistic-psychedelic tactics that extend perceptual sensitivities through the cracks in all of our supposed structural limitations.

V) Stabilisations of power can be punctured at strategic moments of recoil and reverberation—a rupturous click—by surprising accelerations and accentuated instabilities. When such moments of disequilibrium do arrive, notions of asymmetrical rhythm and vague intensity become pertinent concepts to deploy — not merely as metaphors for events reducible to familiar concepts, but as uncertain, operative processes of play during transitionary periods.

Many scoff at such formulations—particularly when things have settled after another disequilibrium. Yet time and again such conservative cautions prove foolhardy. We inhibit a cosmos of heterogeneous, interacting force-fields moving at different speeds. Creative cosmic events—outcomes that are less than chance and more than simple determination—flow through subjectivities rather than being simply reducible to a property of holistic agents.

Metamaterialism renders immanent the separations between human and nature, synthetic and natural, virtual and real. As morality is based in anthropic sovereignty, all moral codification are thus invalidated by an immanent ethics grounded on local causal affects. The idea of extrinsic laws governing material actions ceases and is replaced by an immanent causality of intertextual self-signification pregnant with infinitely incomprehensible possibilities.

an introduction to a fractal ontology

"All of my propositions serve as elucidations in the following way: anyone who understands me eventually recognizes them as nonsensical, when we have used them—as steps—to climb beyond them. [We] must, so to speak, throw away the ladder after [we] have climbed through it." -Ludwig Wittgenstein, Tractatus Logico-Philosophicus, 1921: 6.54.

All relations are founded upon the simple yet indispensable truth that in the beginning there was noise, not silence. Even the simplest words arrive much later—and at any rate, words are still noise. In his illuminating work on The Parasite, philosopher Michel Serres reminds us that the primary grounding of noise is chaos: the pure multiplicity behind things, without any pre-existing order or organisation. The indefinite presence of noise means no system is without turbulence for very long, that there is always chaos, multiplicity and deviation—in short, ontology is always parasitic, always a background noise, always a depth and darkness beyond the flows between order and disorder.

All knowledges are an attempt to bring order to noise—to forcefully organise the chaos continually fixing everything together in an asymmetrical block of concurrent becoming. We can call this instantaneous zigzag a fractal ontology—a set of concepts and categories that show the properties and relations between them. The following is an introductory exploration of some of the phenomenological implications of such an ontology—of the vital mutations of becoming that operate as a material intensification of existentialism, a thorough going-beyond of Martin Heidegger, an exploration of Friedrich Nietzsche's maps, as well as declaration of war on Aristotle, Descartes, and Kant.

We will deploy a number of over-simplified examples to clarify these points. Importantly, these shouldn't be taken as arguments, rather they are tools that will help us think about the terrain upon which a fractal ontology is situated. One of the biggest challenges here is that a fractal ontology is an attempt to write in a space beyond analogy—far past what Franz Kafka refers to as the ceaseless constraints of the metaphor—and against the smooth categorisations of language. In other words, a fractal ontology does not give examples (A is like B), or define terms cleanly (A is any X that has such and such properties) because that would defeat the purpose. Like Wittgenstein's ladder, these examples are merely tools to move us to a space where they are no longer necessary.

the problem of demarcation

Imagine that you're eating a pear. This seems like a simple 'event:' you, the subject, are eating, verbing, the pear, the object. There are two things, you and the pear—thanks to the laws of syntax, the verb 'eating' quickly tells us who's dictating the relation.

When we try to define these things further, we quickly run into some difficulties: where's the 'cut off' for the pear, as in, where does the pear end and begin? In everyday life we tend use the notion of geometrical space occupied by the (transparent) flows of oxygen as a convenient measure for demarcating objects. So the pear ends at the yellow skin, and the bite mark. However, this is obviously just a pragmatic and intuitive short hand at the macro level—Gilles Deleuze and Felix Guattari refer to this level as molar. Surely we can find a more 'objective' edge by zooming in to this edge and drawing up a line.

As we zoom in to the edge of the pear, though, a nice clear line doesn't reveal itself— like a fractal (ontology), the edge becomes more and more ambiguous. We discover that other things are eating the pear too, that the skin is porous, that chemical reactions are exploding off it. We find that our bodies (hands) are effortlessly transferring energy as heat into the pear, which is causing other imperceptible (macro) chemical shifts.

Now that we are 'zoomed in' these tiny transformations in the pear are huge. Around the bite mark there's even saliva, containing our DNA, bubbling and transforming the sugars in the pear and reacting with the acid, with particles flaking off and floating through the air in a cloud being sucked up through our noses—so now even the supposedly simple question of 'where does the eating begin and end' is beginning to get really blurry.

We can call this problem the demarcation problem. And while you might think that this ambiguity (of the object) is essentially meaningless (uninteresting?), for all pragmatic intents and purposes we have no trouble defining where the pear ends and we begin— we're doing metaphysics, so it is interesting and problematic, and, more importantly, where a pear ends and begins in a geometrical space indeed isn't a problem very well suited to cause us worry, but where a person begins and ends in a political space is.

If we just use pragmatic 'edge-marking' techniques we haven't problematised the issue of who is marking these edges, and for what pragmatic function. We mark the edges of the pear like this so we can coordinate our bites, and not eat our hands, which is obvious enough, but when we mark the edges of something like 'woman/man,' 'normal/ abnormal,' 'sane/insane,' 'permissible/perverted' these demarcations can have huge consequences. This is doubled when we consider that the demarcations are merely a method for creating regions on a cloud of molecular elements distributed chaotically for some pragmatic ends (again, what ends?) and then begin to use the demarcation as primary, mistaking the map for the territory, as it were: 'here is, naturally, the binary of men and women, and they are all such and such; you're either one or the other, etc…'

Thus a fractal ontology begins against the modes of thinking that mistake the map for the territory, and don't question the political, social, cultural, and administrative aims for which these maps are expedient. Anyone who has realised that a country is more than geopolitical lines on a map, and that lines on the map signify nothing but a specific set of ideas, not a permanent geographical feature, has intuited this demarcation problem.

Yet it is important to point out that mistaking maps for territories isn't some special or deficient case. We're always dealing with and manipulating maps because language is a cartography. Thus maps, once drawn, are not merely sterile descriptions of the world (as is), they are also ontologically performative upon the 'molecules' they organise.

Have you ever met someone who eats the core of a pear? It makes a difference to the genealogy of the pear whether the core is eaten or composted or discarded. We can see this in the history of agriculture and cultivation: pears have been getting bigger and

18

sweeter over millennia. It's not, strictly speaking, the pears' collective concern or desire to continue becoming bigger and sweeter, it's the concern of the (socio-linguistic) maps we have drawn that pears have become ensnared by and thus subsumed under.

the tree yellows

How do we think beyond maps with their static regions (being)? According to Deleuze's The Logic of Sense, the trick is to start thinking of verbs as primary. Verbs are often seen as less substantial than nouns (or adjectives) because their mapping is more chaotic. If you've studied a foreign language—French perhaps, with its 20 or so different verb tenses for conjugating the past, present, and future—you'll know this all too well.

We can transform the proposition 'the tree is yellow' to 'the tree yellows.' The process of yellowing is more fundamental than yellow—referring to an unfurling event from which we derive the static theme 'yellow.' Making this shift renders certain metaphysical problems about objects and their properties less problematic. By A Thousand Plateaus Deleuze and Guattari have gotten to 'a-treeing yellows.' That is, they are turning static 'beings' (regions on the map with their properties allocated by definitions that demarcate their edge points) to 'becomings,' 'doings,' 'transpirings.' In other words, we are confronting the molecules squiggly shifting under the molar territories on the map.

There are no people, only 'personations' that begin and end (this beginning and ending are transformations), with the in-between—a life lived—being some sort of 'semi-stable' state representing the crossing of some threshold at some critical point. The transition from ice to water to steam is a useful analogy here because we can grasp these transformations but they are anything but smooth or linear—the properties, capabilities, and possibilities of ice, steam and water differ drastically, and they can change rapidly (sublimation, evaporation, condensation, etc.) depending on the state they occupy.

Billions of personations bumbling and stumbling around, persistently personating before deadening and then decomposing. All around this giant cloud of personating we draw a region of best fit, call it 'person,' and develop various methods for describing and reaffirming this line—methods such as our DNA convergences, commonalities of phenotypical expression, commonalities of commercial function (i.e. occupation), commonalities of stances towards (this is how to properly say 'hello'), legal jurisdictions (private property, state boundaries), etc. Obviously such maps have nothing to do with personhood, or with the a-personating that's a-going on around here-ish. The definition 'person' is static and dead. This map has to do with personation—a process that is persisting in a semi-stable state underneath the fixed definition of 'person' and thus it can find a new semi-stable state (evolution) or destruct (extinction).

In The Genealogy of Morals, Friedrich Nietzsche reminds us: there is no 'being' behind doing, effecting, becoming; 'the doer' is merely a fiction added to the deed. Things only seem like things (discrete objects) because we have some pragmatic interest in treating and demarcating them as such in a given context (field/map), and this is mirrored in and enforced by language. What's more, though ensnared by the methods with which we demarcate them, things aren't really concerned with the maps we have drawn—they blur and bleed out of the borders. A person is a person until the critical threshold of the transformation into inert flesh and static organs. Our name for this threshold is death.

19

Thus things (being), are just features of maps we draw. Beneath them are transforming, semi-stable processes of becoming (Doing! Effecting!). In these transformations, our semi-stable states (person) are book-ended by critical points these processes stumble into, over, and out of—representing a fundamental transformation in that things/persons only seem like things/persons (discrete objects/subjects) because we have a pragmatic interest in treating and demarcating them as such within a given context (field/map).

assemblages of the unconscious

When we look at a person's teeth—remember, teeth are 'teethings,' that is, the sucking up of calcium and deployment into a semi-stable tooth shape/ state that is itself engaged in a constant process of decaying and resisting decay—we can only understand them by looking at what a person eats. Those pearly whites are rapidly yellowing. But why are they 'teething' like that? Too much black coffee and red wine? Not enough brushing?

Teeth are teething like that in the same way that flesh is 'fleshing.' The tooth and the skin of the pear blend and bleed into each other in the 'biting.' The biting is another becoming, another thing we've mapped (separated) out. But the biting only makes sense when taken in conjunction with tooth and pear skin (and stomachs, hunger, food, supermarkets, pear trees, etc.). So people have teeth and stomachs and hunger and prey with skin and seeds and sugars in orchards with hills and grass and wind and smells, and in different maps we can create a myriad of regions to demarcate all of this in a myriad of different ways. But underneath all such maps these (fractal) entities bleed together and hold each other in semi-stable states between thresholds—a temporary assembling of particles (teeth, seeds, hills, wind, etc.) that form into an assemblage.

If it is still necessary to talk about structure (being) in relation to an assemblage—which is not self-evident—we could say that it is structured like an unconscious machine fuelled by a multiplicity of modes of semiotisation (of which linguistic enunciation is by no means the most important). It is on this condition that one can remove the shackles of the subjective, consciential, and personative limitations through which desire and the unconscious have been imprisoned. An assemblage is neither individual nor collective, and they exist everywhere that a labour of significations bears on reality in such a way so as to constitute or demarcate a vision/map/productive perception of the world.

Why are snow leopards fast? Because jackrabbits are fast. Why are jackrabbits fast? Because snow leopards are fast. The leg muscles of the snow leopard and the leg muscles of the jackrabbit are both a single 'becoming-fast' resonating in a semi-stable state (assemblage), but they are also connected up, obviously, to a 'becoming-prey-becoming-predator,' a bit-ing, a hunger-ing, a flee-ing and a chase-ing (the leg muscles mean nothing unless there is chasing and eating). Using one map we can demarcate this

20

semi-stable state as 'the cynegetic process,' using another we can demarcate it as 'an ecological balance,' and using another we demarcate it as 'Planet Earth, S01E03.'

It is also important to note that even though the legs of the snow leopard and the legs of the jackrabbit are a single interconnected assemblage of 'becoming-fast,' the snow leopard and the jackrabbit obviously have different quantitative speeds. It is too simple to say that the jackrabbit is as fast as the snow leopard and the snow leopard as fast as the jackrabbit—the relationship is asymmetric and multifaceted. Thinking about this should help us appreciated how many disparate elements, geographies, temperatures, protein fibres, hormones, neurones, behaviours, tendencies, causes and effects, all get tangled up in this one assemblage of 'becoming-fast.' What's more, we must remember that all of these entangled 'things' are not static objects or properties 'belonging' to the snow leopard or the jackrabbit, they too are becomings, resonating in semi-stable states between thresholds, entangled together in a chaotic myriad of intertwined assemblages.

not imitation but transformation

In Civilization and its Discontents, Sigmund Freud's great innovation was the discovery of tunnels underneath our maps connecting disparate (unconscious) regions, whereby a snow leopard, for example, can simultaneously connect the subject to a father, while at the same time concealing that connection. Yet Deleuze and Guattari claim Freud hasn't gone beyond the assumption that regions on a map are beings, and their connections (through the subconscious) are lines of signification. They want to flip this picture upside down, where signifying a snow leopard becomes a becoming-snow-leopard.

Now as we have said, becoming-snow leopard is not the same as imitating (signifying) a snow-leopard, but bringing the particles that constitute one's body—what one merely is—into arrangements with the assemblages that make up becoming-snow-leopard: the semi-stable states/processes humming along in the region we have loosely demarcated as 'snow-leopard.' We've already pointed out that a person's (or a snow-leopard's) tooth forms an assemblage with a prey's skin and a biting, and a (…), so imitating a snow-leopard on the plane of resemblance (maps) (i.e. filing my teeth down to points so they look like snow-leopard teeth) is not the entirety of 'becoming-snow-leopard,' that would be just me (region a) signifying a snow-leopard (region b), not becoming-snow-leopard.

Actors can help us think about this. When an actor needs to play the role of an alcoholic father, despite being neither, it's not merely enough to read a few articles about the two topics. Better to find one (an alcoholic father) and imitate their gait, their tone of voice, their flush, and their way of holding their body. Yet better still is to go within oneself and find those particles that already are part of the assemblage of 'alcoholic father beats their children,' the disappointment, the aggression, the sadism, the masochism and surplus enjoyment, literally become the becoming-alcoholic father, raising the intensity of these points over thresholds to create a new organisation (assemblage) of the body.

Imitating a given example, or set of given examples, will always be confined to the demarcated map regions, resulting in pantomime, gestures, and movements that signify the alcoholic father through the logic of the mapping procedures (region a signifies region b). Becoming one doesn't mean literally becoming an alcoholic and having children—it's about making the particles one is resonate in semi-stable states in the site of the assemblage alcoholic-father.

Acting is not at all about imitation, it is about transformation. Growling like a snow leopard is different from growling as snow-leopard:

> *"Do not imitate a dog, but make your organism enter into composition with something else in such a way that the particles emitted from the aggregate thus composed will be canine as a function of movement and rest, or of molecular proximity, into which they enter,"* Deleuze and Guattari, (1987:302).

Think of the becoming-animal of the warrior. The fighter jet is not supposed to resemble or even imitate the snow leopard, but is painted in line with the becoming-snow leopard, becoming-animal, of the soldiers flying it. It's one outward symptom, or trace, of the transformation they are trying to enact on themselves, on what they are becoming. Making oneself a snow leopard doesn't necessarily mean 'go into the tundra and stalk and eat jackrabbits.' The field of molecules we map into the region 'snow leopard' enter into all manner of assemblages: biting, killing, terrifying, running, sleeping, hunting, bleeding, becoming-invisible, becoming-explosive, nightmares, horror movies, etc.

To say 'the soldiers desire to become snow leopards' is also inaccurate, because this is always going to be an imitation, because we have already expressed two distinct beings (soldiers and snow leopard), two distinct map regions. But if we remember the map is secondary, that 'soldiers' and 'snow leopards' are a pragmatic distinction we make upon a chaotic distribution of particles, we see that the two regions, sharing particles between them in any given map (field), can enter into subterranean singularities and alliances.

To take up an ontology that is fractal in nature we must accept that there are no soldiers or snow leopards, just particles forming various assemblages in semi-stable states of becoming that we then use some method or other to demarcate into regions: this bunch of stuff is a soldier, and that bunch of stuff is a snow leopard. For example, we can write a poem charting a new map, one where a snow leopard stares at a photo of its sweetheart back home and a soldier tracks the smell of blood over half of a mile. This is what Deleuze and Guattari mean by 'becoming-other,' this slipping beneath the maps and seeing the multitude of assemblages that compose the 'beings' on the map's surface, and thus realising they are fractal and can be formed and blended together.

locating our metamorphosis-machines

As any political engagement with the concept of becoming-other is only ever going to be a territorial approximation, we need to look at a fractal ontology in relation to our ability to obliterate and to reconstruct maps. For Deleuze and Guattari, war machines—engines of differentiation that we will instead refer to here as metamorphosis-machines—are the processes through which we expunge and reassemble maps. [1] We should also remember that 'machine' in Deleuzo-Guattarian thought simply refers to a combination of forces or elements—it does not have any overtones of instrumentalism or of mindless mechanisms. A social group, an ecosystem, a knight on horseback are all 'machines.'

By initiating a process of deterritorialisation—a Deleuzo-Guattarian term for the means through which something departs/breaks from a given territory or map—metamorphosis-machines function as a form of social assemblage directed against the ways of thinking in terms of stasis, sovereignty, and being. The way such machines undermine traditional understandings of ontology as static is by exercising diffuse power to break down concentrated power through the replacement of 'striated' (i.e. regulated, marked) space with 'smooth' (i.e. fractal) space. For example, think of how street gangs communicate to resist subordination by rival gangs, or how autonomous social movements—such as the European squatters' movement, the Zapatistas, the networks of protest against summits or the everyday practices of indigenous groups—resist concentrations of political power.

In other words, the metamorphosis-machine—the force through which we can fractalise ontology—is a space characterised by pluralities, multiplicities, and differences, which escape traditional-coding by eschewing binary structures. On the ground, we might even say schizoanalysis is the political embodiment of such processes. For as Serres reminds us, the metamorphosis-machine is the noise—whatever escapes capture, a cross-signal or lawless irruption witnessed in the chaotic permutations introduced by becoming-other.

Metamorphosis-machines help us think in terms of a theoretical terrain characterised by conceptual openness to plurality and difference that eschews stable identities, essences and conceptual unities that form fixed assemblages. Such machines are what make possible the transformation of the soldier into snow leopard, the pear into teeth, the tree into yellow, the actor into alcoholic father, or the living into dead. Such a becoming-other involves a return to what Deleuze and Guattari call a 'fibroproliferative unground' that allows us to begin a project of strategic affirmation of any becoming whatsoever: becoming-woman, becoming-child, becoming-animal, but also other even more strange becomings: becoming-machine, becoming-molecular, becoming-cosmic, etc.

One only need to think of the intensity and of the self-obliterating passion at the opening of, for example, a new romantic affair to grasp these 'too great a diversity of conjugated becomings' that are brought into play through the metamorphosis-machine of love. Out of the intensity of a new relationship, semi-stable identities form in the wake of the destruction, and in the end you have a new assemblage that we refer to as 'love.'

The very passion that founds the relationship also works to destroy these stable regions of gender organisation by creating a myriad of unexpected assemblages (loving-arguing- living-dying-going-thinking-becoming-animal-becoming-pear-becoming-metamorphasis-machine). Once again, the demarcation problem comes to the fore as the members of the relationship obliterate each other in a cloud of molecules—bleeding out and over and under any map that tries to fix and impose upon them static, individuated mode of being.

In politics—as in loving, eating, playing, etc.—we can rebuild maps that determine our unfolding however we wish (of course, these constructions and re-constructions always exist in relation to the specific material conditions of socio-economic life). Hence why it's utterly monstrous when, as under newly-minted President Trump, the traditional political, social, cultural, familial, biological, and metaphorical maps that have kept us imprisoned in false categories of power (by subjugating genders, races, classes, etc.) are restored unchanged, imported wholesale from somewhere extraneous to the present moment.

From problems of demarcation and personation through to assemblages of animality and gender, the world exists in/as a fractal ontology. Of course, this cursory introduction shouldn't be taken as a static argument so much as an assemblage of tools to help us to start building new metamorphosis-machines in order to confront and reassemble in a political space beyond the limits of tradition, being, and analogy—far past the ceaseless constraints of the metaphor and against the smooth categorisations of language. From here, the task of augmenting logics and mutating binaries to move through the current configurations of power is now (and has always been) yours to take up.

> *"We don't know yet what the multiple entails when it is no longer attributed, that is, after it has been elevated to the status of the substantive," Deleuze and Guattari, (1987:04).*

part II. schizoanalysis

25

the disintegration of the masses and the rise of the schizohistorian

We showed America that the silent majority is no longer silent. Today, we created an America that WINS again. Today, we made our hopes, our dreams – our limitless potential – an unequivocal new reality. Today, we made history. Today, we created a government that is once again of, by, and for the people. — Donald J. Trump. American President-elect, Victory Speech, November 8, 2016.

According to their imaginary representation, the masses drift somewhere between passivity and wild spontaneity, but always as a potential energy, a reservoir of the social and of social energy — today a mute referent, tomorrow when they speak up and cease to be the 'silent majority', a protagonist of history. —Jean Baudrillard, In the Shadow of the Silent Majorities. New York: Semiotext(e), 1982:2.

For those with a political agenda, the people are always the hero, the victim, or the chief obstacle. For those on the modern political left, the masses are the victim suffering from false consciousness but are also a latent hero. Thus, the revolutionary can awaken this fettered colossus and stride into the next stage of history. Or, when these projects fail, the people are the ignorant masses who remain enslaved due to their narrow vision of the world. For the modern political right, the masses can be a useful political ally—one that must be disciplined and talked to on a level they are assumed to comprehend like a child that does not know its own strength.

The idea of the masses is a useful starting-point, a solid immovable barrier that we cannot pass through: "the whole chaotic constellation of the social revolves around that spongy referent, that opaque but equally translucent reality, that nothingness: the masses," (Baudrillard, 1982:1).[1]

Our inability to dissect the mass into classes or discernible categories shows the flaw in our idea of the social. Our desire to study society, to have a science about human life, meets its match here. Instead of finding a subject for study, the modern project of social science crashes into this unmovable, unknowable first particle, the masses. All of the work of social science is confronted with the fact there is no discernible object of study, just a black hole which engulfs the socius.

This impenetrability of the masses and their rejection of elite cajoling, is an intentional reaction against meaning. This is a fundamental point that has been overlooked or deliberately ignored. The tendency in modernity is always to lament the ignorance of the docile masses. But there is nothing to deplore within the masses supposed indifference to political events, history, art, and culture and everything to analyse as the brute fact of a collective retaliation and of a refusal to participate in the recommended ideals, however enlightened the political elites say they are.

Yet, social thinking does not take this observation as its starting point. Rather than facing this truly important point, the social and political sciences discard the issue by asking instead how to enlighten this poor victim. This quest to 'enlighten the masses' has led to the social sciences' devising various methods of contact: surveys, polls, and tests. This maneuver has extended the life of the social and political because the masses do, after all, exist. However, as recent unexpected events have reminded us once again, the representation of the masses is no longer possible in an impossibly complicated world that is at once, entirely liberated from coherence.[2]

Politics has been forced to rely on simulations of the people as a substitute. The media reports to us through newscasts what various shades of liberals, conservatives, socialists etc. are thinking. The masses that do exist are not engaged but simulated, poked and probed by the technologies of social science. No longer being under the reign of will or representation, the politics of everyday life falls under the province of diagnosis, or divination, pure and simple—whence the universal reign of information and statistics. No longer a participating subject, the masses are simulated for the political class to engage with through the media and probed for signs of their desires, hopes, and fears by social scientists working in the academic machine.[3]

As an endless spectacle channeled through the hands of Donald Trump has made clear, the so-called silent majorities in contemporary society are not interested in facts and in seriousness.[4]

Although our society is good at creating and manipulating consumer demand, our technicians of social science, our titians of globalization, and our political leaders have failed to stimulate the demand for meaning. Or, perhaps we should say, the demand for any particular meaning. In other words, the people have become a public. It is the sporting match or film or cartoon which serve as models for their perception of the political sphere. The people enjoy the everyday, like a home movie—the fluctuations of their own perceptions in the hourly release of opinion polls.

Nothing in all this engages any responsibility. And it is from this perspective, this vulgar and violent realisation that we must all think more deeply about the history of political activity and its possible replacement. Maybe this replacement can be a political project that takes a new form.

Perhaps its replacement is a different form of social activity for contemporary societies that addresses the questions once answered by politics. In either case, we must move to devote more effort to investigating what the masses are concerned with. Rather than maintaining this fiction that the majority is silent through ignorance, we, with the impetuous to act, need to accept that the masses' unexpected turn in their politics must first be understood if it is to be overcome.

Instead of cajoling some sample group into choosing an answer from one of our ubiquitous surveys—thus creating the simulated public once again—we should be investigating what the masses are doing without such provocations. This task demands a schizo-historical approach toward thinking about politics and society. With a methodology of thick description, we may find new intersections of social activity that can replace the modern political forms we have inherited.

To revive politics, we need to find an alternative to the current, dominant strategy of mass political behaviour—an alternative to the now looming silence that Baudrillard (1983) describes.

> I) Schizohistory answers when new forms of radical energy call for a new materialist history. In the study of the schizophrenic motivations of events both actual and virtual, the schizohistorian attempts to combine the insights of schizoanalysis with the research mythology of the social sciences to understand the schizo-somatic —emotional, affective, visceral—origins of the social and political behaviour of the masses in our past, present, and futural materialist conditions.

> II) Schizohistory derives many of its concepts from areas that are perceived to be ignored by conventional historians and psychoanalysts as shaping factors of human existence, in particular, the apparent anxious, nihilistic affects of the post-modern condition— an increasingly collective realization that all life is constructed by a material, unpredictable, and contradictory muddling of meaning, all meaning is constructed by power, and ergo that all reality is constructed by power.

> III) Schizohistory requires a commitment to probe the affective, aesthetic, and algorithmic dimensions of the silent majority within post-fact capitalism—a technocratic echo chamber in which facts have now been jettisoned from our political reality—to engage and

mobilize past, present, and future experiences of people towards a Levinasian socio-ethical transformation.[5]

IV) Schizohistory discards the mass Cartesian self-other distinction by articulating a monistic connection between alterity and singularity through reflecting on the other's resistance to comprehension, which is expressed in subjectivity—the most comprehensive site of normativity, but it is neither its origin nor its source. Instead this ethical subjectivity can only be thought of as difference in-itself.[6] Subjectivity cannot be universally described or represented, since it is not a phenomenon with particular qualities, presented in the context of a horizon, positioned in relation to other objects, and so forth—and yet, it is also not a mere abstraction or mystical apparition. Rather, subjectivity has an ethical meaning—it presents itself us as the irreducible presence of a mortal and vulnerable other with whom we are a social relation, whether we like it or not. This presentation already expresses the command not to murder—it already conveys an ethical resistance which puts our powers in question and asks us to justify ourselves. In this sense, subjectivity is actual more than virtual/visual—it commands and calls for a response.

V) Schizohistory depends on the idea that, since one cannot, in a Kantian sense, universally locate the non-reducible desires of subjectivity in the actions of a particular individual, an affective study of the masses can help to better understand the general flow of future events.

This politico-ethical obligation put forward by schizohistory is not about securing some sort of grounded and incontestable moral certainty in precariously uncertain time—the demand for schizo-ethical justification is not issued once and for all in a momentous encounter with the stranger, but that it is renewed at every moment, in every conversation with every other.

Instead, what we must do is deploy a schizohistoriography that works to expose the simulacra of the masses and find forms of political activity that cannot be so easily simulated. Doing so requires expanding our categories of analyses to include the affective phenomena of the postmodern condition. It is in this bewildering but provocative terrain we are likely to find more fertile counterpoints of resistance to the political simulacra that the silent majorities disdain.

on a futural materialism

Considering this history in which there are so many disorders, so many oppressions, so many unexpected things and turnings-back, there is nothing which predestines it for a final harmony.

There is a fundamental chance in history, an adversity which hides it from the grasp of the 'strongest' and most 'intelligent' of people. And if they finally exorcise this evil spirit, it is through no transcendent principle but simply through recourse to the givens of our condition.

With the same gesture we must brush aside both hope and despair. If there is an adversity, it is nameless, unintentional.

Nowhere can we find an obstacle we have not helped create through our errors or our own faults. Nowhere can we set a limit to our power. No matter what surprises the event may bring, we can no more rid ourselves of expectations and of (non)consciousnesses than we can of our bodies.

Complex societies—which means more-than-human societies at scales of socio-technical organisation that surpass phenomenological determination—are those in which the past, the present, and the future enter into an economy where maybe none of these modes is primary, or where the future replaces the present as the lead structuring aspect of time.

In other words, time is folding. We are not just living in an accelerated time, but time itself—the direction of time—has changed. We no longer have a linear time, in the sense of the past being followed by the present and then the future.

Thus there are multiple materialist historicities.

One of them is ironic—even derisory—explicitly historical and made of misinterpretations, for each age struggles against the others as against aliens by imposing its concerns and perspectives upon and towards them.

This history is forgetfulness rather than memory—it the dismemberment of a forceful silence, an ignorance, externality.

But another history, without which the first would be impossible, is constituted and reconstituted step by step by the futural interest which bears us toward that which is not us and by that life which the future—and/as the past—in a continuous exchange, brings to us and finds in us, and which it continues to lead in each maker who revives, recaptures, and renews the entire undertaking of making new works.

30

a phenomenological encounter with schizoaesthetics

superstitions, illusions, hallucinations, and phantasies are not limited to an alternate realm of psychic 'reality' as Cartesian mind-body duality. desiring-production is the process and means through which the (collective) psyche produces links, connections, and associations between thoughts, feelings, ideas, sensations, and memories that construct and re-construct meaning. these meanings, produced by desire, are not 'things' but nonetheless material 'objects,' part and the whole—a monistic maneuver through dialectical thinking. schizophrenics are aware that they do not share the same iterations of 'reality' as everyone else, but we see this as a failing in the construct of the 'individual' rather than a flaw in subjectivity. in a de-nihilist (an non-ontologically inherent) reaction to this, we move to develop a method of thinking about art-practice as a form of de-schizoanalysis (what we call schizo-aesthetics)—attaching the prefix 'aesthetics' to activate a schizoanalytic practice that moves away from capitalism's clinical-analytic framework, therapeutics, and the clinical and ecological responsibilities and problems raised by the therapeutic and socio-political contexts neoliberal subjects are forced to work within. if the schizophrenic (as diagnosed by the clinical-analytic field of psychology), sees their long dead mother in the room with them, they do not question whether this is possible or not—we can say precisely the same about us, the schizo-aesthetics, who see the mechanisms of the society of control (illusion manifesting as anxiety), or conversely, the aesthetic dimension (de-illusion actualising as creativity) as a space for resistance-as-absurdity (for resisting and resisting resistance, for ontologically inherent contradiction, for de-nihilism)—they aren't troubled by any such doubts. this is the essential difference between de-illusion (schizo-aesthetic) and illusion (psycho-analytic). what de-illusionals (schizoaesthetics) see is what *is*, quite literally (the multiplicity of existence, desire as creativity) the initiative object (which is material) becoming actualised (and/but also not only, the hyperreal, the virtual), a becoming-revolutionary that is productive, a radically fulfilled desiring-production (this breaking from the capitalist simulacrum, not in a transcendence, but in an immanence, a rupture in that it is still constituted by capitalism, but on a new frequency, in a new way, which in its un-familiarity [its' non-familial, anti-oedipal nature an assertion that psycho-geographies are irreducible to universal and transcendental oedipal structures, a non-totalising critique of transcendental values there is a theatrical de-consciousness held hostage by the factory of consciousness], its absurdness, has highly subversive qualities—it confronts and renders immanent the problem of the immanent critique in that it is obviously a reaction to the hyperreal, the simulacric ontological violences of the de/re-territorialising tendencies of capitalism, but at the same time it deploys its own de-simulation [grounded in the ontologically inherent contradiction of de-nihilism] which collapses the virtual and the real [revealing the monadic, non-dialectical nature of existence which itself is perhaps best ruptured by the treatment of difference as multiplicitous within itself—it ruptures the externalisation of 'difference between' and 'difference from' by enframing internal difference, pure immanence, 'A LIFE's'] and produces 'rupturous subjectivity's' that can take stock of the current functions of assemblages under capitalism [look to the non-dialectical distinctions of Felix Guattari: social subjection molar, individualising, territorialising and machinic enslavement molecular, dividualising de/re-territorialising]—subjectivities substantiated by difference, de-substantiation ['de' in the sense of 'de-nihilism'] which perform a genealogy of [the violences of] capitalism while also creating) initiated by moving (fluidity, process) to conceptualise desire as productive—in other words, to treat desire as an actualisation (and/but not exclusively a virtualisation) of the performance of desire (a performance in the theatre of the absurd, the theatre of cruelty, which moves to jar, to obfuscate, to metamorph [to deploy ontologically inherent contradiction the river is always changing, is a commitment to a transvaluation of all values, an epistomology of anarchy, flux, change, immanent difference in and of itself, or better yet, themselves to problematise the violence of transcendence, the static nature of Platonic forms, to introduce a process philosophy de-grounded in a pataphysics which moves to take nothing seriously, and thus take seriously, nothing—the micro-physical and micro-political, that accelerates the inherent contradictions of the de-territorialising maneuvers of capitalism by actualising presently captured subjectivity])—this is the becoming-revolutionary potential of schizoaesthetic in capitalism's perpetually re-territorialising supraliminal illusion—an open, post-art collectivity.

31

"The best way to keep a prisoner from escaping is to make sure they never know they're in prison." - Dostoyevsky

SAN FRANCISCO
Meet your minimum wage replacement

HELLO, MAY I TAKE YOUR ORDER?

BEG FOR SCRAPS OR YOU WILL STARVE

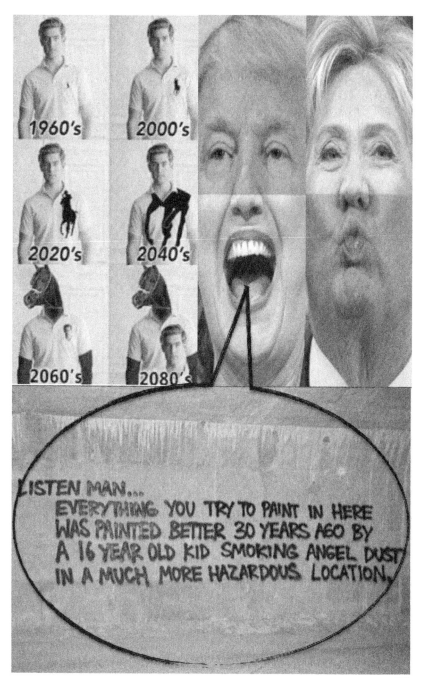

33

a theory of
technoanarchism

This work charts the speculative relationship between technology and anarchy. What follows is not a proposal for a 'coherent' political system. Rather, it is a sketch of some vital ideas on epistemology, technology, and politics that speak to processes of experimenting with the digital mediums of a rapidly accelerating Internet age. This techno-genetic turn towards the rhizomatic underpinnings of technology is about venturing out into the world of objects, material processes, vibrant matters, technological and cosmological time. What this work attempts to put forward is a means to make sense of the multiple crises that we find ourselves faced with; to think through the materialities of power to better understand the subjugating processes of capitalism.

As a result, it puts forward a meso-politics of contingency, a set of technoanarchistic pragmatics that include but are not limited to: *decentralisation, open source, anonymity, contingency, and absurdism*. Running through it are discussions of epistemology, subjectivity, integration, techno-genesis, nonconsciousness, and anarchistic forms of resistance. For technoanarchism, this resistance comes through new cartographies of speculation—a *reductio ad absurdum*, a meso politics of immanence that problematises not only social laws, which we see as corrupt, stifling, and transient, but moral, physical, and perceptual laws as well, all in order to envisage a post-representational political moment no longer tied to stimulated desires in a control society.

keywords: *reductio ad absurdum*, techno-anarchism, meso-politics, techno-genesis

introduction: speculation and technoanarchism

Early in 2016, a self-described 'independent, radical' publisher sent out an email. The email, which was vainglorious titled: 'Psst! Downloading Isn't Stealing [for today],' advertised a number of ebooks for free download in honour of the release of a newly published collection of writings by computer programmer, writer, political organiser, and open-source hacktivist, Aaron Swartz.[1]

The subject line alone is troublesome to anyone who followed Swartz's life and politics closely—in January of 2013, facing 35 years of imprisonment for downloading over four million academic articles with the intention of releasing them online for free, Swartz committed suicide at the age of 26. Moreover, Swartz's book, *The Boy Who Could Change the World*, was unavailable for download, as the publisher 'did not have the North American rights' to realise the writings online.

Ironically, not only does the email implicitly condemn downloading as stealing—on most days—but Swartz's book, a book written by an open source activist who took his own life in the fight for free and open information online, was hidden behind a licensing paywall—the very same type of paywall that Swartz was relentlessly charged with 'data theft' for breeching at MIT back in 2011.

The publisher's inclinations represent a serious lack of understanding for the types of principles that Swartz was fighting to uphold. And while the perspectives that follow here are not explicitly representative of Swartz himself, they speak to a larger techno-anarchic *ethos* that he worked his whole life to develop.[2] An ethos that—if the aforementioned email is any indication—is gravely misunderstood in both popular media and 'critical,' 'radical,' and 'progressive' spaces.[3]

This work represents an anarchistic attempt to address this knowledge gap. What follows is by no means a coherent system—no form of anarchism ever is. Rather it is a sketch of some vital ideas on epistemology, technology, and politics initiated by people like Swartz that speak to an interest in combining the new technologies of the digital age with active experimentation in order to confront the violent territorialisations of daily life in a hyper-industrialised capitalist society.

Such a speculative turn towards the anarchic possibilities of technology are about leaving the comfortable waters of human narcissism behind and venturing out into the world of objects, material processes, vibrant matters, geological and cosmological time, and thus simultaneously enacting a philosophy that rediscovers the more-than-human ecologies that we are embedded in. What this work offers is a means to further probe the multiple crises that we find ourselves faced with, to think through the materialities of power, to trace the cartographies of capitalism.

Key to such works are the common desire of leaving behind the tired distinction between nature and culture in ways that avoid reproducing the modernist trap of treating the world as separate from humanity—some raw material 'out there' that can be ceaselessly territorialised as our own inexhaustible means to freedom. By articulating how we are embedded within technologies and are ourselves processes of technological subjectivity, technoanarchism explodes through the constraints of endless framings around discourse, language, power-knowledge, textuality, and culture. What follows is a discussion of the possibilities—epistemologically, technologically, and politically—engendered by such realisations, in the hopes that we can not only appreciate what people like Swartz continue to fight for, but can contribute to this ongoing struggle in new ways.

epistemology and technoanarchism
The hallmark of technological anarchism is its steadfast opposition to all the established orders of things: to the state-form, the capitalism system, and the ubiquitous institutions and ideologies that de/re-territorialise these structures into a control society.[4] The habitual neoliberal order must be destroyed through an overcoming not merely of our social circumstances, but of the physical world—an overcoming of modern epistemology.[5] We deny not only social laws, which we see as corrupt, stifling, and transient, but moral, physical, and perceptual laws as well—we envisage a mode of existence no longer tied to the stimulated desires of socially subjectivised individualism.

knowledge as epistemologically anarchic

Like the Dadaism that we draw from, this anarchistic epistemology resists congealment into any single programme, including its own.[6] Feyerabend: "To be a true Dadaist, one must also be an anti-Dadaist," (1975:266). Given an aim, we may approach it with help from organised groups or more dispersed collectivities—we may use reason, emotion, ridicule, even 'an attitude of serious concern' to confuse rationalists by inventing compelling reasons for unreasonable doctrines.

There is no view, however 'absurd,' we refuse to consider or act upon—no method is regarded as wholly indispensable. The one thing we oppose positively and absolutely are universal laws, universal standards, and universal ideas such as 'truth,' 'reason,' 'justice,' and the behaviours they bring along. Following from the *reductio ad absurdum* of Feyerabend (1975) and others, we take great interest in procedures, phenomena, and experiences which indicate that perceptions can be arranged in discombobulated and unusual ways, and that the choice of a particular arrangement as corresponding to 'reality,' while not arbitrary—it always depends on traditions—is certainly not more 'rational' or more 'objective' than the choice of any other arrangement.[7]

Since absolutely nothing can be predicated with any certainty as to the 'true nature of things', all projects, as Nietzsche (1882) points out, can only be founded on the 'nothing.' Yet *there must be a project*—if only because we ourselves resist being categorised as 'nothing.' Out of nothing we make something: an uprising, a revolt against everything which proclaims to know the nature of things. We disagree, we are 'unnatural'—out of nothing, techno-anarchic epistemology provides a means to imagine new values, and by this act of invention, move to create unfamiliar worlds.

No systematisation, according to a technoanarchic epistemology, has a legitimate right to 'exist.' All ontological claims to a metaphysical transcendent are spurious, except the claim of chaos—which however is undetermined. Egalitarian forms of large scale governance are impossible, for as Bey (1987) points out, any form of 'order' we have not imagined and produced directly and spontaneously in sheer 'existential freedom' for our own celebratory purposes—is an illusion.

Underneath this shifting and ephemeral un-positioning lies the staunch conviction there are no exception-less methodological rules governing knowledge and information. For as Feyerabend (1975) reminds us, the history of knowledge is so complex and convoluted that if we must insist on a general methodology which will not inhibit the fluid and chaotic nature of existence, the only 'rule' that it can contain is the epistemologically anarchic proposition that 'anything goes.'

Such dispersed and post-representational conceptions are loosely assembled by the realisation that we will cease to be enslaved by the cautious conformisms of traditional organisations of knowledge and information only when we render immanent our most fundamental categories and convictions—including those which allegedly make us 'human.' Thus the realisation that reason and anti-reason, sense and non-sense, design and chance, consciousness and non-consciousness, intentionality and un-intentionally all flow together as co-constitutive parts of an informational assemblage are vital points in all epistemologically techno-anarchic approaches.

anarchic subjectivities as fluid, dispersed

Whether in its conception of politics—*Who is the 'subject' of politics? Who can change things?*—or in its radical nature—*Who can rebel? Who can liberate themselves, and liberate themselves from whom or what?*—epistemological anarchism conceptualises subjectivity as multiplicitious.

For a techno-anarchic epistemology, fixed 'subjects,' meaning 'individuals' as free, unchanging entities who are responsible before themselves and the world, are a most *primarily repressive ordering of things*:[8] from that of Plato and the *forms*, Descartes and the *cogito*, and Kant and the *transcendental subject*, to that of liberal humanism, the Enlightenment and French Revolution, of the 'the rights of man and citizen,' of Adam Smith and the 'free market', law, modern, secular morality and the hollowed out nature of what we presuppose to be representative democracy.[9]

In contrast to this static notion of the modern subject as unified, continuous, and homogeneous—existing in one form, duplicated by as many copies as there are individuals—epistemological anarchism conceptualises a radical subjectivism, fluid, dispersed, and chaotic subjectivities that are multiple, changing, and heterogeneous. Their forms vary constantly in size and quality. They are always collective, and regard the individual, in the commonplace sense, as a largely illusory figure—a manifestation of capture and control that takes on many convincing metamorphoses.

Technological anarchism seeks to counter the *micro-political* controls over life through a coming together of subjectivities working against a myriad of subjugations.[10] We are not at all groups of individuals, we are assemblages of enunciation—non-denumerable units of desiring-subversion, which cultivate our preferences for randomness, fluidity, hybridity, and a repudiation of vanguard tactics. As Guattari (1989) continues, we are a deepest affinity for affinity, for non-universalising, non-hierarchical, non-coercive relationships based in a commitment to chaotic dispersion. What we deploy is difference, the project of working ourselves towards affirming a groundless ground.

Although thinkers such as Nietzsche (1878, 1882), Foucault (1966, 1969), Deleuze and Guattari (1983, 1987) do not explicitly identify as anarchists, their ideas are of great importance given the post-representational nature of their thought.[11] Through them, the grounding for epistemological anarchism comes in to view: *an anarchism of becoming*, which does not have an eventual goal, nor does it flow into 'being,' it is not a final state of development, nor is it a static form of society, rather, it becomes permanent only insofar as it continually represents a means without end.[12]

Thus when thinking through the vital nature of reality, epistemological anarchism points to the ongoing process of 'subjectivation,' to the 'plane of non-consistency' through which fractured, dispersed, chaotic, and anonymous subjectivities can be (re)formed.[13] As Colson (1996) points out, such epistemologies are neither an ideal, nor a utopia, nor an abstraction. Epistemological techno-anarchism is neither a program, nor is it a catalogue of regulations or prohibitions. It is a force common to all beings which expresses the immanence of the possibilities all these beings contain, a living subjectivity which, in certain circumstances, takes us outside of ourselves.

technology and technoanarchism

As we move deeper into a highly technological regime in which the infrastructures surrounding us become more complex, it is increasingly apparent that the epistemologically techno-anarchic subjectivities operating on a plane of non-consistency can never be conceptualised in isolation from various systems through which we are in constant and constitutive interaction. The notion of 'human agency' as paramount is illusive. We reject such anthropocentrism by recognising the distributed nature of subjectivity among human and non-human entities—certain technological, biological and social processes predispose and channel more traditional 'human' actions.[14]

the potentialities of integration

Philosophers of technology such as Simondon (1958) and Stiegler (1998) assert that humans have always been integrated into their environments and have co-evolved with them. In their form and operation, information technologies have always constituted our social, political, and economic relations—they are not mere coefficients, but direct effectors of the territorialisations of capitalism.[15] In other words, technological mediums constitute a global society, not merely by the messages and signifiers they deliver, but by the characteristics of the mediums themselves—the integrated meanings of technical forms are inseparable from the forms' social content.[16]

The present form of information thus induces a certain type of social relation—assimilative to that of the capitalist mode of production. What is new about the present moment however, is the unprecedented degree with which we can actively build and change these relations. With such developments in mind, technoanarchism points to the the fact that these technologies also contain, by virtue of their co-constitutive structures, an immanent, multiplicitious, and anarchic 'co-logic' of communication—energy and information systems as co-subjectivations with the potential to break precisely from the politicised opposition between consumption and production.

In other words, by enabling new feedback loops and new forms of amplification between human evolution and technological developments, the Internet simultaneously constitutes the possibility for implementing new distributed and decentralised networks of subjectivities—the potential for a plane of non-consistency that dissipates the reductive hyper-industrial binaries of input-output.

Think of the massive drop in the cost of the production of technologies, data transactions, and the replication of technical materials—both analogue and digital—as Stiegler (2014) points out, this has given contemporary society the ability to acquire 'new practical competencies,' but also 'analytical and reflexive competencies,' which are essentially the possibilities of those situated outside the nexuses of power to develop skills, abilities, or functionalities—different modes of dispersed subjectivation—that had previously been restricted to more exclusive social spaces.

Indeed, according to Marx's (1939) analysis of the division of labour—the division between the professional and the non-professional, between the master and apprentice, the bourgeoisie and proletariat, and so on—in a pre-digital, pre-Internet system, the possibilities opened up by the spread of information were far more limited. Thus technoanarchism points to the fact that the fluid nature of socio-digital technologies creates new, dispersed channels of meaning-making.

What is necessary, is therefore to create systems for producing metadata that organise and create political technologies based on, not just collaborative bottom up systems—as these can be essentially top-downed by the *culture industry*[17]—but genuinely heterogeneous and anarchic methods through which the existential articulation of differing perspectives and critiques can be rooted—one that moves through the systemisation of a hyper-industrial, consumerist, capitalist epoch, in order to reach new anarchical modes of existence—modes that enable our multiple expressions of subjectivity to establish new forms of analytic critique through which the digital realm can start to separate from the spectre of the hyper-industrial capitalist political economy.

technogenesis and nonconsciousness

Digital technologies have vastly expanded our ability to communicate, research, compile, share, and organise information while newer interfaces continue to techno-genetically integrate us into these processes. Take the techno-genetic mutation of human attention. As Hayles (2012) points out, humans are equipped with deep and hyper attention. Deep attention has a high threshold for boredom and enables engagement in a specific task or problem over an extended period of time, while hyper attention requires constant gratification and yet enables the quick scanning of significant amounts of data in order to gain an perspective overview or identify certain problems.

Now, with the development of our ubiquitously networked digital devices, we occupy a socio-technical environment that systematically privileges hyper attention. This has profound effects on cognition, and as Hayles (2012) notes, such an ontogenetic adaptation actively reconfigures the technical environment in a direct way that requires more hyper attentiveness—we invent things and they invent us, we co-evolve. If we think of this process in terms of what Hayles calls *technogenesis*, we can see there is not necessarily a change in the biological structures of the brain, but an ontogenetic change through which technologies rewire subjectivities as we grow.

39

With digital technologies we have the capacity to capture and process unimaginable amounts of data—from a technoanarchist perspective, this has both advantages and disadvantages. While events like the *Snowden Affair* have made it clear that these technologies enable new forms of surveillance and control that were unthinkable prior to the emergence of the Internet, through processes such as technogenesis, we can see the re-coding of socio-biological assemblages in exciting new ways. For example, beyond merely altering attention spans, as Guattari (2010) and Lazzarato (2014) point out, in order to filter the increasing amounts of information we are forced to process, we are seeing a very drastic expansion in our techno-cognitive nonconsciousness.

Such non-conscious processes—distinct from the unconscious defined by psychoanalysis[18]—filter the enormous amounts of information coming from the body and the environment through sensory perceptions. Recognising patterns, drawing inferences, adjudicating between conflicting and ambiguous information—as Hayles (2012) observes, we are learning that increasingly, our bodies react entirely non-consciously to external stimuli, a behaviour that we share with many contemporary technical systems in a technogenetic feedback loop of informational production.

In approaching questions of knowledge, subjectivity, and integration from the perspective of this technogenetic feedback loop, technoanarchism highlights the ways in which, as Guattari (2010) claims, we are living in a techno-centric universe—where the semiotic machines of economics, science, technology, art, and so on, function in parallel, and non-consciously as they produce or convey meaning—in this way, they bypass anthropocentric significations and representations.

The existence of such technogenetic processes means that we can no longer employ more traditional models of communicative and information theories,[19] in which exchanges are realised between individualised subjects through emitter-receptor/sender-receiver analogies. Instead we must think in terms of 'inputs and outputs,' 'machinic assemblages,' 'technogenetic mutations,' all of which have less to with 'human' and more to do with our technoanarchistic subjectivations.

politics and technoanarchism

Epistemology as anarchic, subjectivity as multiplicitious, technology as co-constitutive, humanity as technogenetic—running through all of these seemingly dispersed rhizomatic outgrowths is a subterranean technoanarchistic co-logic, a non-reductive monism that moves to un-ground the ideological and material assumptions underpinning the apparatus of the autonomous humanist liberal subject. What this un-grounding attempts to open up is a space for a new kind of techno-anarchistic meso-politics—a networked, anonymous, and de-individualised space where the pragmatics of resisting the terrain of capitalism are alive, vivid, and much more difficult to co-opt or destroy than they are at the micro (i.e. individualised) or the macro (i.e. globalised) register.[20]

the pragmatics of resistance

As techno-anarchism insists that we cannot know in advance which way a line of flight is going to turn, we see politics as a speculative process of active experimentation. This spirit of ongoing experimentation is our grounding, our means to an endless end. We are not interested in the militant elitism of vanguardist politics. Instead, in establishing a nuanced pragmatics of resisting, technoanarchism moves to spread the seeds of rupture that trigger uncontrollable moments and deterritorialisations of the dominant political paradigm by way of contagion and propagation.

We must always be wary of looming tendencies to congeal into fixed partisan movements that merely reproduce and expand the hierarchical inequalities and individualised subjectivities of neoliberal capitalism. Instead, to propagate a politics of non-co-optation, we must, as Simondon (1958) notes, prime our interventions within a dispersed and fluid state of transversal becoming.

Such interventions depart from the basic mantra that 'information wants to be free.' We assign this statement a deeper meaning beyond the simple observation that 'information *should* be free.' For techno-anarchists, technology possess an internal chaos, a potentiality, which makes it vitally incompatible with privatised and regulated notions of proprietary software, copyrights, patents, and subscription services. Channeling a technogenetic ethos, we see information as a dynamic entelechy, an evolving force that cannot be contained within any ideological structure.

This is not to say that the Internet itself currently has an anarchic architecture. There are many well cited texts in multiple fields charting the regulated nature of Internet protocols, (for example, Galloway, 2004). Moreover, the ways in which the Internet functions as an apparatus of the control society is becoming more and more apparent with every new surveillance revelation and Wikileaks cable. What technoanarchism gestures to is not some techno-utopian understanding of the Internet as an entirely free and open space, but to the ways in which epistemologies and subjectivities can operate anarchically on the Internet by engaging in techno-genetic means of becoming —subjectivities that establish dispersed and anonymous forms of expression through which the digital may be able to break from the social and machinic subjugations of capitalism.

For example, *Usenet* is one of the earliest applications deployed on the Internet, preceding the modern Web by over six years, it is a peer-to-peer network of open-source computing based on principles of net neutrality, open communication, and user anonymity.[21] Like *Freenet*, *Entropy*, and the *I2Ps* that followed, Usenet has no central server or dedicated administrator, rather, it's a constantly changing conglomeration of servers that store and forward messages to one another.

As a peer-to-peer network is designed around the notion of equal peer nodes simultaneously functioning as both 'clients' and 'servers' to the other nodes on the network, this model differs from a client-server network arrangement, where communication is usually to and from a central server. For technoanarchism, such peer-to-peer networks embody the dispersed, co-constitutive and multiplicitious anti-logics of transversal communication—as a result, they actively alter the capitalist mode of production by breaking from the opposition between consumer and producer.

moving to disperse the datascape

While technoanarchism shares the same deep affinities towards net neutrality and free, libre, and open source software (FLOSS), it can be distinguished from other more libertarian forms of crypto-anarchism—which tend to emphasise personal privacy via encrypted communications between individuals. Instead of attempting to hide from surveilling and corporatising practices of the state-market assemblage—an unsustainable long-term practice as no level of encryption is indefinitely secure—technoanarchism is about creating new, open, accessible networks and communities of dispersed users based on the vital principle of a ubiquitous right to information.

Constructing a new pragmatics of the digital, one that deepens our techno-genetic mutations, requires more than just a commitment to privacy—a commitment which tends to be couched in a liberal humanist rhetoric of the individual: 'my privacy,' 'my data,' 'my information,' 'my rights,' and so on. In order to actualise the chaotic, multiplicitious, and co-constitutive nature of techno-anarchism, we advocate for a speculative meso-politics of ephemeral, contingent pragmatics.

decentralisation: following from the architecture of peer-to-peer networks, technoanarchistic acts are *decentralised*—lacking in central servers, leaders, or any dedicated administrators.

open source: keeping in line with our deep commitment to drastically expand the presence of FLOSS, whenever possible, we utilise, advocate, and share *open source* software programs.

anonymity: drawing from our conception of subjectivity as anarchic and dispersed, we remain *anonymous* whenever possible in order to avoid being reduced to a single, static identification.

contingency: guarding against the temptation to congeal into fixed, vanguardist movements, we practice a politics of *contingency,* insisting that our actions disperse as quickly as they form.

absurdism: returning to our Dadaist routes, we deploy *absurdity,* parody, mimicry, mockery and other tactics to create 'playful' politics that may appear 'harmless' but are in fact very effective.

Such a technoanarchist politics draws from the tactics and theories of a number of anarchist and hacktivist traditions. Too many to name in their entirety, they include post-anarchism, the Situationists International, cyberpunk, schizo-analyses, Marxist autonomism, the Chaos Computer Club, and Anonymous. What ties these seemingly disparate movements together is their shared interest in combining new technologies with active experimentation in order to confront the violent territorialisations of daily life in a hyper-industrialised capitalist society.

These are not confrontations that are meant to take place in the shadows, on the peripheries. In order to spread the seeds of rupture necessary to trigger uncontrollable moments of resistance and realisation, the speculative politics of technoanarchism manifests out in the open, they are participatory, inclusive, and playful, contingent, decentralised, and anonymous— things that the structures, despite promises to the contrary, are not—and on present course, can never be.

Of course, these are not rigid dictums and this is by no means a final and comprehensive treatise. In keeping with the creative, contingent, and fluid departures of technoanarchism, we must always be questioning, amending, and improvising. Take these ephemeral pragmatics and collaborate, build, create, manifest, pull apart—then share it, disseminate it, throw away those neoliberal desires for credit and recognition. Make the action the return. For the ones who take up technoanarchism in it entirety, are ones who open up its pure potentialities in new ways.

conclusion: control and technoanarchism

Wikileaks' Cablegate, the Snowden Documents, the Afghanistan War Logs, the recent Panama Papers—if massive leaks such as these are any indication, we are living in a highly securitised and surveilled political climate—a diffuse matrix of new information gathering algorithms, where information is tracked and ordered into patterns deemed either acceptable or unacceptable.[22]

By rendering information in this way, our society of control maintains an illusion of freedom. We are 'free' to say and do what we want—within pre-circumscribed desires. Since the only forms of discourse prohibited in the media assemblage are radical indictments of our political system and calls to 'terrorist' or insurrectionary action, most of us fall within such parameters without even thinking about it, and so experience ourselves as free to express our views and live our lives.

When, like Aaron Swartz, we fight for increased open access publishing and creative commons licensing, or 'simply' attempt to dump publicly-funded knowledge into spaces where the public can actually access it, we see the true face of capitalism as unbridled control. It does not matter if we really are being watched at any moment, the point is to normalise the feeling we could be.

After all, we know that we are being tracked. Touch off enough markers in Internet activity by going to certain sites or using certain words and you will be placed on a 'watchlist.' Rather than being spurred to paranoia by this, we are encouraged to relax, while at the same time asked for confidence and endorsement of the idea that those who are breaking the rules will be caught. It is this latter idea—that 'wrongdoers' should and will always be caught—which technoanarchism forcefully calls into question in an attempt to pose a sustained challenge to the matrix of control.

Inadmissible behaviours are largely unrecognised as existing, or situated under the category of the 'criminal,' a concept we rarely take the time to call into question. As a result, a divide is created—a class that falls outside the 'we' who have freedom—and deep thought about the shared subjectivity of these 'categories' is strongly discouraged. We are under control precisely to the extent we think of those subjugated to the effects of power as anything other than 'us.'

In reality, there is no grand authority to overthrow, no sovereign, not even an explicit disciplinary program—control manifests at the every day register. We are slaves to our desire—or rather, it is desire that is being enslaved. As Debord (1967) points out, resistance thus involves refusing to desire the forms of knowledge being sold to us. Desire must become open and creative—we need more differentiation, a rejection of binaries, and a refusal to separate subjectivities out into 'Selves'—the 'free' populous—and 'Others'—criminals, activists, hackers, immigrants, etc.

The challenge is how we imagine a world we inhibit. For technoanarchism, resistance comes through speculation, a *reductio ad absurdum*, a meso politics of immanence—taken up out of nothing, it momentarily fuses, ridicules, subverts, and dissipates just as quickly, before it can be monetised, stratified, individualised. Perhaps then, we can say that the contingent pragmatics which inform resistance are the most important part. After all, technoanarchism does not order the solution beforehand, but is committed to the disordering process of always working towards it—while simultaneously realising that 'it' can never be fully achieved—for 'it' must constantly be pushed further and further if we are to avoid simply reproducing the re-calcifications of control.

live at the pacific national exhibition

spoonfuls of meat!
we're in a beer garden prison.

does your art sell a lot?
there's so much shit here.

there's a lumberjack show we can watch.
there's an angry birds universe.

if you want to go for a smoke we can go for a smoke.
you don't have to lie to me.

an abundance of tinfoil,
but we need to have lunch first.

we need to place a bet:
under 7?
or over 7?
what do you think?

want to check out the fun centre?
gambling for children.
we lost it all on mini roulette.

an army camo visor,
with a matching army camo backpack,
bringing pan-asian food to the streets.

jimmy's lunch, established 1989;
owned and operated by jimmy's children and grandchildren.

they're throwing beach balls in the crowd,
it gets them all excited.

let's go superdogs!
alice pooper; ma-dog-ma; dog racing is corrupt.

even the screams are recordings.
and the people continue to be tortured with noise and lights.

45

'and' as a force of creative stammering

"The tree imposes the verb 'to be,' but the fabric of the rhizome is the conjunct- ion, 'and... and... and...' this conjunction carries enough force to uproot the verb 'to be,' to establish a logic of the AND, overthrow ontology, do away with foundations, fully nullify endings and beginnings," —Deleuze and Guattari,(1980:25).

Rational cognition is modelled on the verb 'to be,' 'IS.' Critical thought is weighed down with insipid discussions about attributive judgements (the sky is blue) and existential judgements (God is) and the possibility or impossibility of reducing one to the other and vice versa. Thus the reductive processes of the conjunctive relations between those who purport to practice critical thought always turns (and then re-turns) back to the IS.

In grounding this dialectic, the IS functions as a discursive contrast buttressed by nothing more than linguistico-material myth, an over-determinacy in search of some sort of incontestable totality. As the means through which we affirm this juxtapositional myth, IS functions as a sleight of hand, an association of an irreconcilable binary opposition with a reconcilable binary opposition—the thesis, antithesis, synthesis triad—creating the inescapable illusion that the former had been resolved.[1]

In turning away from the multiple we incessantly fumble around for the one, the 'to be,' the 'IS.' Critical thought never locates both class AND indigeneity. Never gender AND technology. Never race AND nature. We fight ceaselessly for a return to that originary desire to lay claim to that final IS (it IS race, it IS class, it IS gender, it IS technology).

But when are able to we see these relational judgments as autonomous, it becomes apparent they creep in everywhere, they overtake everything.[2] In contrast to the IS, the AND isn't even a specific conjunction or relation. AND brings in all relations. There are as many relations as there are ANDS—AND doesn't just upset all relations, it upsets the possibility of being, of verb, of metaphor, and of transcendence.

AND, "and...and...and...and..." acts as force of creative stammering, a foreign use of language, a line of diversity, a flow of multiplicity, and the utter dissolution of identity.

In this sense, diversity and multiplicity have nothing to do with aesthetic wholes (in the liberal sense of hiring 'one more minority') or dialectical schemas (in the sense of 'one produces two, which then produces three'). In those cases we are still imposing Unity, still imposing being, still imposing some expectation that the end will bring us to IS.

When we say that everything has two parts—for example, in a day we say there's morning and evening—we're not saying that it's one or the other, or that one becomes the other. Multiplicity is never located in the reduction of meaning to the IS. Multiplicity can be precisely—and perhaps exclusively—located in the AND—a force of difference-in-itself that is unique in nature from the elementary components and collections of IS.

If AND is neither a component nor a collection, what is it? AND what can it do for us?

The force of creative stammering lies in living and thinking and presenting this AND in a very novel way, in making it work actively. AND is neither one thing nor the other, it's exclusively in-between, between two things. There's always an in-between, a border, a line of flight or a flow, only we don't see it because it's the least perceptible of things.

AND is this borderline—a line of flight—along which social transformations may come to pass, becomings evolve, revolutions take shape. Strong positions are never on one side or on the other.[3] To exercise control, power may be directed through an ontology—through an IS—but power always rests on the border—at the AND.

In taking up the force of AND we position ourselves at the precipice of new possibilities for critical throught—we see the fringe, show the imperceptible. In finally turning towards the creative stammering of AND—which connects all thought at the borders of critique— we augment the processes of radical politics by charting a diverse, multiplicitious terrain that upsets all relations by engendering the possibility of a permanent in-between-ness.

Indigeneity AND class, nature AND race, coloniality AND gender, biotechnology AND migration, AND so on. An imperceptible border separates them, belonging to neither but carrying both forward in their disparate development, in a flight or in a flow where we no longer know which is the guiding thread, nor where it's going. A micropolitics of AND.

At this border on the in-between is where a new politics comes to pass. By augmenting forms of thought based in IS, AND operates as a radical device. Rather than assuming tensions away with claims about necessary hierarchies of forces, some comfortable 'horizontality,' or one version of 'postism' or another, AND stretches thought across the borders. Poulantzas AND Guattari. Deleuze AND Trotsky. Lenin AND Haraway. Gramsci AND Benjamin. Materialism AND Postmodernism AND Feminism AND so on.

For augmentation is not about leaving the old and new worlds behind but expanding the range of factors and forces. There IS no END to the political. There are only ANDS. Or rather, there are Ends—vital shiftings of the terrain of politics—AND in the face of such Ends, AND is the force of creative, collective stammering under which we must unite if we hope to confront the crises of political legitimacy thought is currently facing.

an introduction to schizoanalysis

why do the people fight for their own servitude as stubbornly as if it were their salvation?

Such an arresting question was first posed by unconventional psychoanalyst William Reich in his 1933 book, The Mass Psychology of Fascism. In the book, Reich makes the case that psychic repression depends on social oppression, and as a result, the modern conception of the fascist state has been taken up not by sinister external forces but internally, by the masses themselves.

In a democratic society, ostensibly, the principles of an idea or a political movement can only be successful if their program bears a close resemblance to the boilerplate expectations of a broad category of individuals. Take the recent rise of far right reactionaries in Western Europe and the United States: someone like Donald Trump is successful precisely because the psychological structures of the American electorate currently coincide with those of Trump and his ideologies.

According to Reich, the masses have not been deceived by someone like Trump, they desire his rhetorical fascistic discourse, and that is exactly what needs to be explained. In an attempt to do so, Reich develops an entirely different way of exploring political control—what Deleuze and Guattari refer to as the first truly 'materialist psychiatry.' For Reich's work concerns itself first and foremost with the psycho-somatic structures that make fascism possible at the outset, and then only secondarily, does he turn to the issue of fascism as a subject for political discourse.

What this means psycho-politically is that the success of a political movement or revolution are dependent on a precedent revolution of the psyche. After all, to tear down a factory or revolt against a government is to attack the effects of fascism rather than causes, and as long as any attack is focused solely on effects, no structural political change is possible. For Reich, what is truly fascistic is our present construction of systematic thought, of 'rationality' itself. If a factory is torn down, but the rationality that produced it is left standing, we will simply produce another factory. If a political revolution overthrows a despot, but the systematic patterns of thought that produced the despot remain, those patterns will repeat themselves in a succeeding government.

Consider the example of surveillance: the Wikileaks' Cablegate, the Snowden Documents, the Afghanistan War Logs, the recent Panama Papers—if massive leaks such as these are any indication, the present construction of systematic thought alluded to by Reich operates in a highly securitised and surveilled political climate—a diffuse matrix of new information gathering algorithms, where our information is tracked and then ordered into categories of acceptable or unacceptable activities. We know that we are always being tracked—touch off enough markers in Internet activity by going to certain sites or using certain words and you will be placed on a 'watchlist.' Rather than being spurred into anxiety by this unnerving realisation, the vast majority of us 'choose'

48

to ignore it, to continue on with existence as 'usual' and as a result, we tacitly give our endorsement to the notion that those who are breaking the rules will be brought to 'justice.'

Inadmissible behaviours are largely unrecognised as existing, or situated under the category of the 'criminal,' a concept we rarely take the time to call into question. As a result, a divide is created—a class that falls outside the 'we' who have freedom—and deep thought about the shared subjectivity of these 'categories' is strongly discouraged. We are under control precisely to the extent we think of those subjugated to the effects of power as anything other than 'us.'

By rendering the world in this way, our society of control maintains an illusion of freedom. We are 'free' to say and do what we want—within pre-circumscribed desires. Since the only forms of speech prohibited in the public discourse are radical indictments of our political system and calls to 'terrorist' or insurrectionary action, most of us fall within such parameters without even thinking about it, and so experience ourselves as free to express our views and live our lives.

The role of a revolutionary politics then, for Reich, is to understand and to further the historical movement of increasing productivity and potential freedom into the larger psychic and social spheres of society, to push through the limitations of effects in order to trace the causes of our undisclosed desire for control in what are touted as free and open societies. There is no grand authority to overthrow, no centralised sovereign power—for Reich, the mass psychology of fascism is such that we have created a system where we are the prisoners and the guards; as a result, our internalisation of this perverse form of consensual fascism is what enables both the proliferation of the surveillance apparatus and discourses like Trump's to come to the fore.

what is schizoanalysis?

For all of his vital insights into the socio-psychological nature of power and control, Reich never adequately addresses his own question. As Deleuze and Guattari point out in their introduction to schizoanalysis, Anti-Oedipus, Reich was content to answer by invoking the ideological, the subjective, the irrational, and the inhabited because he too remained a prisoner of effect. In other words, Reich fell short of the materialist psychiatry that he dreamed up because his project overlooked the multiplicitious functions of desire in the fascist personality under capitalism.

Drawing from the work of Nietzsche, Marx, and Freud, schizoanalysis is a revolutionary political process that seeks to expand upon Reich's materialist-psychiatric critique of psychoanalysis so as to include the full scope of multiplicitious social and historical factors in its explanations of cognition and behaviour in order to map and thus undermine the causal groundings of fascism.

Schizoanalysis has acquired many different definitions during its development in the philosophic works of Nietzsche, Artaud, Deleuze, and Guattari, as well as literary figures such as Aldous Huxley, William Burroughs, Henry Miller, and Jack Kerouac. What connects these thinkers as schizoanalysts is that they have been able to uproot themselves from the social's causes and traditions in order to conduct physical exoduses from the ideological territories that harboured them through much of their previous lives. Furthermore, each of them is in tune with heightened degrees of empathy and perception—they have been able to focus their gaze on something and tease out the intangible in it—an intangible that transforms something within each of them.

Indeed, literature is akin to schizoanalysis in the way that there is no ultimate goal, no attainable summit that it is reaching towards, and in itself it is only a process, a production of something. A previously held fact is destroyed by each of these authors: for Huxley, it was the deterioration of an anti-psychedelic political climate, for Burroughs, it was the destruction of traditional norms of control, and for Miller and Kerouac, it was the ability to explode the bourgeois morality system.

In a similar manner, the schizophrenic, even in their delirium, finds themselves 'tuned in' to things around them:

> *'It's a given that in the practice of institutional psychotherapy that the schizophrenic who is most lost in himself will suddenly burst out with the most incredible details about your private life, things that you would never imagine anyone could know, and that he will tell you in the most abrupt way truths that you believed to be absolutely secret. It's not a mystery. The schizophrenic has lightening-like access to you; he is focused, so to speak, directly on those links that constitute a series in his subjective system.'* [1]

In many ways, this description of the interaction between the therapist and the schizophrenic is reminiscent of philosopher Peter Sloterdijk's answer to the question 'where is the individual?': "First of all and most often it is part of a couple." [2] This is not just a physical couple per se, though it can take on this form; it is the coupling with the 'self' and the 'other,' various manifestations of alterity that the self relates to. The 'individual' becomes a question of space, but a non-physical space of 'inbetweenness' situated at the fluctuations between one thing and another. Thus Deleuze and Guattari's understanding of the schizophrenic experience, and one of the essential aims of schizoanalysis, is a proliferation of the interconnected state of all things in order to cultivate a 'break' or fracture that allows the entity we mistakenly refer to as the 'individual' to make a jump, a leap onto the plane consistency where processes of becoming can take place.

One asks: How is the schizophrenic able to so lucidly articulate the inner-workings of the self before them? Because they deterritorialise themselves right down to the flows that actually create the individual. For schizoanalysis, schizophrenia is not seen as the disease or mental disturbance that characterises or defines schizophrenics. Schizophrenics as clinic patients—and schizophrenia as a reductive psychiatric diagnosis—result from the vital incompatibility between the dynamics of schizophrenia unleashed by capitalism and the reigning institutions of society.

To be clear, schizoanalysis does not romanticise asylum inmates and their often excruciating and exploitative conditions of existence—conditions which are directly fostered by the 'mental health' institutions proliferated by capitalism. As opposed to an individualised psychological 'problem,' schizoanalysis re-conceptualises schizophrenia as a broad socio-historical system of control that results from the generalised production of psychosis and anxiety that are currently pervading capitalist society—a process that no single psychiatric patent could possibly embody.

In brief, capitalism fosters schizophrenia because the quantitative calculations of the market replace meaning and belief systems as the foundation of society. In this approximation then, we can define schizophrenia—both in the psyche and the socius—as a form of 'unlimited semiosis' that emerges when fixed meanings and beliefs are subverted by the cash-nexus under modern capitalism. Hence, schizophrenia constitutes an objective tendency of capitalist society and its historical development. By way of the simultaneous elimination of extant meanings and beliefs, every extension of capital—from the geographical (imperialism) to psychological (marketing)—manifests as a new layer of the perpetual state of alienated fear: "All that is solid melts into air."[3]

According to Deleuze and Guattari, the powerful capitalist counter-tendency to the emancipatory potentials of schizoanalysis—the driving force behind the resurgence of neo-fascist propensities in democratic states—is paranoia. For if we understand schizophrenia to designate an unlimited chain of semiotic signifiers—radically fluid and extemporaneous forms of meaning—paranoia, by contrast, designates an absolute system of belief where all meaning and all representation is permanently fixed. As a result of this ubiquitous paranoia, we perceive desire, that is, 'what we seek,' as a lack, a reaction, a void—something that must be constantly filled and refilled. Under capitalism desire is commodified, it becomes a libidinal economy—a prison in which what the libido seeks is temporarily satiation enabled by the further commodification of all facets of life.

For schizoanalysis, the terms paranoia and schizophrenia point to what Reich overlooked in his initial materialist-psychiatric critique of power: they are the fundamental organising dynamics of a capitalist society. Paranoia represents what is archaic in capitalism, the resuscitation of the obsolete, rigid, belief-centred modes of social organisation. Whereas schizophrenia embodies capitalism's positive potentials: freedom, ingenuity, and permanent revolution. Hence the schizo-moment is the ultimate subversion of paranoiac systematisation, of the desire to 'build walls,' to draw up psychological, ideological, and material borders between 'us' and 'them.' In deploying a highly figurative style of discourse that manifests in the development of concepts such as 'desiring-machines' and the 'body-without-organs,' schizoanalysis erodes the stifling distinction between metaphor and metamorphosis. In opposition to the paranoiac traditionalism of fascistic thought, schizophrenia's potential for radical freedom designates a revolutionary objective tendency of capitalism that opens up spaces to re-code the flows of desire in new ways.

'Rather than moving in a direction of the reductionist modifications of desire, which merely simplify the complexes of modernity, schizoanalysis works towards its

51

complexification, its processual enrichment, towards the consistency of its virtual lines of bifurcation and differentiation—in short towards its ontological heterogeneity.'[4]

What most revolutionary politics lacks is a new psychology, an anti-psychiatry that will help us to undertake the task of gradually releasing our over-coded flows of desire from the grips of fascist ideologies without sending us straight into a mental institution. This is the primary aim of schizoanalysis: to take the preferable tendencies of schizophrenia to its limits in order to rupture the paranoiac foundations of modern capitalism. Indeed, to push through the limits imposed by capitalist alienation, to replace our position as poor, defenceless, guilt-ridden puppets in internal straight-jackets, with free, non-Oedipalised, non-individualised, uncoded subjectivities. In short, schizoanalysis is move towards taking up the limitless potentials of conceptualising schizophrenia as a revolutionary breakthrough rather than a psychological breakdown.

a schizoanalytical politics

Schizoanalysis is not a psycho-political theory so much as an attitude towards the world. It moves to complicate the paranoiac distinctions between theory and practice, nature and culture, ideology and materiality, self and other, subject and object—to multiply ways of thinking about repressive significations such as race, gender, and class. When speaking of the masses' desire for fascism, it is not enough to focus strictly on the ideological effects of exclusionary rhetoric: as the example of surveillance makes clear, we must also probe the causal structures of power.

For the schizophrenic is someone whose active desire is not regimented, not hierarchicalised by the family, church, school, army, work, etc. Following from this schizo-break, desire for Deleuze and Guattari is seen as productive, affirmative, an active, non-referential flow. Contrary to the paranoia of capitalism, there is no lack here. There is revolutionary-production: desire-producing desire, energy producing energy—our desire as the power to create rather than to consume.

'Desire does not "want" revolution, it is revolutionary in its own right, as though involuntarily, by wanting what it wants… [5] [For] as Marx notes, what exists in fact is not lack, but passion, as a 'natural and sensous object.' Desire is not bolstered by needs, but rather the contrary; needs are derived from desire: they are the counter-products within the real that desire produces. Lack is a counter-effect of desire; it is deposited, distributed, vacuolized within a real that is natural and social.'[6]

Thus contrary to the casual rendering of desire as lack under the paranoiac frame of capitalism, schizoanalysis is a call for the affirmation of desire as open and creative—we need more differentiation, a rejection of binaries, and a refusal to separate subjectivities out into 'Selves'—the 'free' populous—and 'Others'—criminals, activists, hackers, radicals, immigrants, etc.

Desire, like capital, should be understood in terms of flows: flows of the visual, musical, political, temporal, and performative. However, there is a catch here. While the flows of desire emanate from inherently rhizomatic creativities—i.e. the surrealistic art installation—the flows of capital emanate from hierarchical paranoia—i.e. the Trump campaign. Like schizophrenia, this double process of emanation is inherent to capitalism. In other words, capitalism works by inscribing and re-directing the flows of desire so that they may correspond with the flows of capital through coded spaces such as the stock market. This double process is the process of deterritorialisation (degrounding) and territorialisation (grounding). Desire is first deterritorialised by capital: allowing certain aspects of the schizophrenic process to manifest and then it territorialises them: whenever there is a danger that the flows will become 'too' revolutionary.

Capitalism can only exist by liberating production, while at the same time, containing it within limits so that it does not explode out in all directions: "The strength of capitalism resides in the fact that its axiomatic is never saturated, that it is always capable of adding a new axiom to the previous ones."[7] From mod to hipster, hippie to punk, as any subculture begins to strike its own eminently marketable pose, its vocabulary, both visually and verbally, is rendered more and more familiar in anticipation of its impending reterritorialisation into the capitalist axiomatic.

The only way to overcome this problem is for the schizophrenic to continually deterritorialise their own forms of expression, so as to make repetition and incorporation impossible. This is what poet Antonine Artaud had in mind when he called for 'no more of masterpieces'—the end of the commodification of political, cultural, and artistic moments and the flow of non-repeatable signs that name make it impossible for the paranoiac system to bring them in to its own body.[8]

'Performance's only life is in the present. Performance cannot be saved, recorded, documented, or otherwise participate in the circulation or representations of representations. Once it does so, it becomes something other than performance. To the degree that performance enters the economy of reproduction it betrays and lessens the promise of its own ontology.'[9]

Thus schizoanalysis is not an entity, not a field, but the performance of revolutionary potential—the process of constantly deterritorialising the socius so that free-form desire can subvert the capitalist formation of paranoia as power—the process through which more and more people move to create less and less commodifiable critiques. But as Deleuze and Guattari are careful to insist, schizophrenia is the potential for revolution, not the revolution itself. After all, it is in the very nature of schizophrenia as free-form desire that it cannot be assigned to any definite goal or end. By way of its staunch opposition to the fascistic captures of paranoia resulting in our psychological internalisation of control, schizophrenic desire is multiple, inclusive, and nomadic.

As philosopher Eugene Holland suggests, the subornation of this paranoid capitalism to a form of desiring-production would entail (among other things), the cancellation of the infinite debt to capital and a return to alliance-based rather than commodity-based social relations.[10] Yet the major hurdles towards realising the revolutionary potential of schizoanalysis stem from the very primacy of desire that makes schizophrenia's desiring-production ripe with liberating potentials.

For what ultimately governs desire—in this case, what gives capitalism its unprecedented power—is the degree of the development of forces or energies that a given form of political sovereignty is able to organise. When compared to all other social forms, capitalism has developed and organised our energies and forces to a historically unprecedented degree. From Dadaism to the Anti-Globalisation Movement, Surrealism to Occupy Wall Street, as the constant de-and-reterritorialisation of countercultural movements makes uncomfortably clear, capitalism has been able to continually re-generate its own revolution precisely because it can 'develop and commodify' our productive forces to a greater degree than any previous social form.

Thus, with Reich's initial material-psychiatric query in mind, we should really be asking: Under what conditions, and in what form, can we imagine a society emerging that would be more vigorous, in terms of the deterritorialisation of productive forces and energies, than capitalism?

For if the perpetual force of capitalism's paranoiac cycle of liberation and containment does not collide with a more potent, less rigid alternative, perhaps a shift will occur only after capitalism's hyper-exploitation of resources has so severely impaired or even reversed its ability to continue developing productive prices and energies that another mode of social relation will show visible signs of doing better.

part III. anxious capitalism

theses on the philosophy of non-history

"The tradition of the oppressed teaches us that the 'state of emergency" in which we live is not the exception but the rule. We must attain to a conception of history that is in keeping with this insight. Then we shall clearly realize that it is our task to bring about a real state of emergency, and this will improve our position in the struggle against the fascist nature of modernity." —Walter Benjamin, Theses on the Philosophy of History

I. In shifting our atemporal focus to futural materialism—a history 'towards the future,' we have cracked open our doom and salvation. We are now in the process of writing a cosmology, sociology, and theology that radiates out from humanity into a technological utopianism. We are scrawling stick images of god and projecting our as of yet inefficient ideals into the void stretched out in front of us. Past experiences and accomplishments no longer accumulate in a momentum that carries us forward. The future is accelerated—it is now 'coming at us.'

II. This atemporal shift towards acceleration—a frontal, transcendent future— creates a modal shift in philosophy which eviscerates etymological and thus philological grounding by gradually emptying language of its meaning. This is called 'novelty' and is symptomatic of a forward-facing temporality. This emptying however is nullified by a return of the repressed, a reservoir of affective expression that we have termed the collective non-conscious. This collective non-conscious is merely the interminable groundswell and tendency of meaning to re-assert itself, to recuperate it's own ground as it were. The ontological impoverishment of symbolism creates a hole in the reservoir of the materio-ideological dualism of post- enlightenment language through which mythology can again thrive. The experience of this emptying process is experienced in terms such as existential crisis, public secret, the death of god, and nihilism—which has reached an acute social and political pitch that is now best characterised as affect management. This atemporal shift of focus is a rupture in post- metaphysics and agency of supernatural and volatile proportions which as of yet, the vast majority of humanity has yet to catch on to because our caretakers are violent corporate titans who manipulate the visceral dimension of subjectivity in order to maintain power.

III. This atemporal shift does not signal a failure of modernity—it does not invoke a return of traditionalism or conservatism, rather it is caused by a fetishisation of the sep tepi (the fabled 'first time' or zep tepi, when gods or aliens, ruled on Earth, the waters of the abyss receded, the primordial darkness was banished, and the human biogenetic experiment emerged from the light) which we call 'History.' History being nothing more than the selective buttressing of institutional events enforced by sustained and institutionalised ontological violence—governments, militaries, organized religions, debt. This lacuna-based selection process benefits only the victors as it has been said, which creates an asymmetry in agency and agentive capacities resulting in a systematic agentive emptying of the body politic while simultaneously creating a brackish surplus of decadent, over-abundant agency, a cancerous capaciousness wielded by an ever increasing black mass of 'entrepreneurial' elites. The call for a return to 'historical' values is thus an unwitting identification with the radiant qualities of sepsis. Symptom decried as solution. History becomes a weaponization of the apophatic which most resembles our own evisceration—a preparation for entombment. History is thus a series of declensions maintained and perpetuated by ever increasing acts of blatant violence. This increase receives patronage by the recent instillation of greed as a virtue, greed as social dynamo,greed as vehicle of the reified deity we call progress. The increasingly blatant examples of violence which threatens monistic, subjective anonymity—the very antithesis of Plato's transcendental, universal soul—is the apotheosis of history's inherently violent nature.

IV. The failure of humanities leaders to instil abilities and capacities to thrive ontologically and metaphysically naturally creates a species wide sickness which grows in it's acute viscerality as time moves 'forward.' This yawning, placid abyss that opens ever wider before us can be best described as infinity sickness. Every where and every when are happening now albeit in a spectrally distorted simulacric revisionism, a propogandic orgy of advertisement. History has invoked it's own enantiodromia by eviscerating the necessary sensorial, affective, metaphysical and thus apperceptive faculties necessary for humanity as a whole to process it's essential 'historyness.' Everyone's dystopia and utopia exist concurrently right now.

V. Infinity sickness is the result of being systematically deprived of 'participatory mechanisms,' metaphysics and agentive techno-logos such as mythology, sorcery, viscerality, and organic cosmology. This is all categorically held within the Cartesian prison we have manifested.

VI. Our current basket of maladies have been intensified and exacerbated by the most recent violent declension that was the copernican revolution—the storm of progress at any cost.

VII. The souls primary purpose in 'advanced' western civilization has been arbiter of temporality, yet the recent shift towards the future with its marching incessant metaphysical and sensorial declensions leads to the the breakdown of this arbitrage function of the soul. This is expressed currently in our shift towards conspiratorial meta-narratives as equally plausible cultural cosmogonies—a post-fact constellation is rapidly usurping the vestigial vestment of more 'grounded' traditionalist creation myths. As politics and religiosity conflate into a degenerative trumping of 'reason,' the return of the repressed first trickles through through the advent of the 'fantasy' narrative. From Harry Potter and The Avengers to Pokemon Go and Game of Thrones—we gorge on impossibly baroque alternative realities which only appear so perpetually fantasmic due to the strict logistic limitations of aesthetico-cultural expression under the invasive entelechy of infinite sickness—that inescapable anxiety which flows through the voyeuristic, scientific, consumeristic groundings of life in late capitalism.

VIII. Thus we enter into a vague experience of the enantiodromiac folding of the endlessing möbius. A looping reversal experienced eschatologically. A walking backwards into the future. A walking forward into history. An angel of non-history. Ancient future scholars again believing that we are the first to find a mummy with an iPhone in its rigomortised clutches.

IX. This ever increasing asymmetry of illusory and non-illusory agencies fluctuating between the rulers and the ruled is not dissimilar to the head telling the body to build another guillotine.

X. Viewed in a pragmatic light, the affect of history is not a philosophy nor a politics. It is not a sustainable nor viable system. It is a cancerous non-system. History is adversarial to Time. History is a time virus. Thus it's proper study is not philosophy or history—it is a pathology.

XI. The virality of time suggests both evolution and re-denigration simultaneously. We are experiencing a scientifico-reductionist birth—further fulfillment of the opera of enlightenment. The black mass of entrepreneurship —narcissistic social phantoms, invalidated phalluses, fabricators who entertain grandiose god delusions on a plane of pure, unadulterated elitism—seek the will to leave, to flee the Earth in order to propagate the galaxy or be swallowed by now silicone sentient matter representing the Earth's immune system rising up to surround, isolate, and dissolve the virus before it can activate it's mutagenic epigenetic capacities.

XII. The immanent failure of humanity, as it currently operates under late capitalism, to leave this planet in the ubiquity of its excrement and toxic soaked environs signals a monistic ethics in the primordial laws governing the ultimate reality of the ontologically chaotic cosmos.

XIII. The survived and successful evacuation of humanity from this planet with all present psycho-pathologies intact, in other words the utilisation of psychopathological reason—an Oedipal late capitalism auto-cannibalistic in expression— to successfully become a truly corporeally 'cosmic' entity would signal the amorality of primal ethics governing reality.

XIV. Thus it can be accurately stated that this planet is simultaneously a prison, a school, a stand-up routine and a playground—at least until Kafka's trial reaches its untimely conclusions. Thus the verdict of "judgement" in the religious sense may be shocking indeed.

XV. The anti-christ and anti-nihilism of the final judgement is the progenitor of accelerationism.

XVI. Accelerationism is the recognition that there is no way out. No escape from the current divulged model of human nature. There is no system that can fix our problems currently and no 'systeming' will do. Accelerationism is the archetypal abjection of systems in total.

XVII. There is no 'logic' nor 'irrationality' there is only logos. There is only thought driven and driving logos—there is no do-er behind Nietzsche's deed. Merely pure process philosophy.

XVIII. Whatever is most taken for granted has the most potency in an agentive capacity, thus the perceived dialectical duality between reason and opinion, material and ideological, is false. There is only one option: creation. Mind is primary as in primal, first. Thus the divisions and discords that we perpetuate and sanction as 'political,' 'religious,' 'scientific,' or humanist are merely subcategories subsumed under the a fundamental ubiquity of processual subjectivity.

XIX. What, then, is after the orgy?[1] If opulence fermented is decadence, what is the ferment of that? An explosion of mediocrity has flooded the sensate and incorporeal that has stimulated a necessary relationship between affect, voyeurism, espionage, banality, and mimesis.

XX. The enantiodromia of our collective non-history— the affirmation of the knowledge of the experience of traversing the infinite möbius—is the key to initiating a rupturing of subjectivity towards infinite creativity. All things, ideas, and institutions become their opposite—a folding in on the plane of pure immanence. This is the logical result of infinitude—a casting aside of the limits of matter, laws of nature, gravity, boundedness, limit itself—within a crucible, a space, a non-history in which we realise post-modernity is a rare reflexive moment that challenges us to refuse to use and abuse history to reproduce power and order once more.

59

Seperation is itself an intregal part of the unity of this world...

on the necessity of destruction

"We must be harsh, cruel, and deceptive to what we love." — Proust

Joy and hatred are not necessarily elements on the opposite end of some spectrum—subjectivity's scream lies helplessly at the very centre of social transformation itself.

Early 2017 has been a jarring re-introduction to this scream. From the hyper-nationalism of Brexit and Trump's increasingly explicit, fascistic, and vehemently Islamophobic turn, to Tartus (Syria), No Lives Matter, and No Hope of Mitigating the Impending Disaster of Global Warming, in 2017, spectral negativities have conjured a surrealist no-ology that has furiously penetrated every facet of our carefree little neo-liberalised imaginaries.[1]

Can we have unmitigated growth and environmental sustainability? No. Can we have tangible equality of socio-economic opportunity and the unprecedented concentration of wealth? No. Can we have less fatalistic international, regional, and communal relations and the relentless proliferation of deadly corporeal or psychosomatic armaments? No.

In a mere three decades, (neo)liberalism's cultural dominance following from Soviet communism's collapse has decayed into a smug complacency buttressed by a violent project of imperialism-masquerading-as-globalisation. Amid growing inequality, society's 'winners' continue to tell themselves they live in an extraterrestrial Elysium—and that their meritocratic successes are therefore deserved. All the while, the experts they have created to concentrate the world's collective economic output in the plump, manicured hands of a few impotent meta-oligarchs continue to marvel at their own brilliance.

Many will recoil in horror at this notion, but thanks to last year's spectacular conjugation of the pessimistic face of postmodernity, the tapestry of the enlightenment's illicit rape of subjectivity (which reduces all socio-political life to a set of discourses that can be managed) has begun to come undone. The rise of a populist right—Brexit in Britain, Modi in India, Trump in America, Duarte in the Philippines—gestures to the unexpected fragmentation of a once impenetrable alliance between the hawkish, entho-nationalist forces of the neoconservative right and the global financial flows of neoliberal centrism.

Thanks to the utter devastation automation and outsourcing have wrought on the poor, white, god-fearing communities of the 'developed world' (processes which they initiated by installing Regan and Thatcherism some 30 years ago), the alliance between the nationalists and the capitalists—an alliance which made possible the social and political flattening of difference by way of globalization—can no longer agree on the best way to subjugate the other. Hate crimes are on the rise as the naked callousness of power devours its young, and as is custom, the marginalized are bearing the brunt of it all.

We can glimpse the negative lurking in plain sight by merely shifting perspective. And when all seems lost, from the bright glow of no-ology's despair we can draw strength.

62

In a world no longer illuminated by the light of God, there are many possible borders between divergent underground worlds. What is the becoming of creativity but the un-becoming of something else, a small evasion of power through destruction-in-itself?

the destruction of worlds

Worlds are destroyed everyday by the market, the police, the military, and even by the do-gooders of philanthro-capitalism—the world itself may very well be eradicated under the ecological forces we arrogantly signify with the term 'Anthropocene.' But all of these things are of the world as it is, because of the world as it is, and it is for this reason that we must not wince at the thought that it is the world as it is which must be destroyed.

To talk of the 'destruction of worlds' is to talk of learning how to say no to this world, to refuse that which it offers and that which it stands posed to say. The spectre of no-ology is an impulse of (non-dialectic) negation which insists that in a world characterized by compulsory happiness, generalized precarity, class stratification, summary executions of people of colour, decentralized control, and overexposure, revolutionary negativity is the only course of action which does not heave us back towards the flaccidity of liberalism.

This liberal flaccidity, where 'belief in the world' signifies the need for a re-connection to the world as it is, the no-ology's necessity of destruction reminds us one should only believe in the world inasmuch as one desires grounds to destroy it—the 'world' must be understood not only as a mass, social hallucination, but as a transcendental illusion.

No-ology is a conspiracy—a conspiracy to keep alive the idea of revolution in counter-revolutionary times by making thought a war machine that breaks the collusion between institutionalized morality, capitalism, and the state. The preliminary materials to do this were prepared by Nietzsche, who wanted to use ceaseless laughter as an experimental instrument to dissolve all identities into phantasms: "since man has never been anything but the unfold of man, man must fold and refold God."[2]

In a time when the death of God and man seem so banal, only the death of the world can be a truly heretical proposition.

Thus in the face of our biopolitical obsession with over-production and over-creation, we must again find an appetite for destruction. This requires the progressive, anxiety-ridden revelation that destroying worlds is not a return to nihilism-in-itself, but the mapping of another way of smashing capitalism, of redefining communalism, and of constituting a war machine that is capable of countering the world war machine by other means.

Writing the disaster of 2017 is how we break free from the stifling perpetual present, for the present carries with itself a suffocating urgency. The present imposes material limits.

In post-modern, post-fact, post-truth capitalism, the past and the future are an empty form of time that exist only through representation—the former in history as the present memorialization of things passed, and the latter in the yet-to-come as the projection of an image of the present. The (liberal) optimist sees revolution as an eminently practical reorientation toward the present achieved while generating a new image of the future. In contrast, the no-ologists learning to hate the world must short-circuit the 'here and now' to play out the scene differently. While still being in this world, they turn away from it.

This is the life of revolutionary characters so shameful they force the world to stand still —Alfred Jarry's King Ubu, Fodor Dostoyevsky's Idiot, William Shakespeare's Lear.

a post-shame terrain

2017 has forced upon us the realisation subjectivity under late capitalism has become a subjectivity of shame. It has grown from the seeds of a composite feeling made from the compromises with our time—the shame of being alive, the shame of indignity, the shame that it happens to others, the shame others can do it, the shame of not being able to prevent it. "Subjects are born quite as much from misery as from triumph."[3]

The events of this year may have brought the concepts of post-truth and post-fact to the fore, but what about the rise of post-shame? How do we challenge a politician who cannot be embarrassed? Or to protest a political system that thrives on the absurd?

To cope with the reality of this post-shame we must probe the origins of shame. For his part, in Totem and Taboo, Freud locates shame in 'the primal horde,' a great band of brothers ruled over by an all-powerful patriarch.[4]

This awful father enjoys all the women in the horde (that is the only role women have in this expectedly misogynistic tale), and leaves the brothers out sexually, to the point where they rise up, kill, and devour the tyrant. Yet this act plunges them into deep guilt (it is the first time it is felt), and so they elevate the dead father again, now as a god, or at least a totem around which taboos are established (the taboos against murder and incest above all). As art critic Hal Foster reminds us in Bad New Days, this shame, for Freud, is where modern society begins.[5]

But why recall Freud's primal father in relation to the post-shame of new populism? It is, after all, hazardous to psychologize anyone, let alone millions of voters, to totalize them in this way. But there is a schizoanalytic dimension we have to probe. No doubt many who are supporting this turn towards totalitarianism are sexist and racist—whether implicitly or not—but most are angry at elites too.

Moreover, they are also excited by Trump and Modi, by Duterte and Brexit— excited to vote for them. They thrive not only on negative resentment but positive passion. A potent double-identification in which new populism means submission to the father as authority and envy of the father as outlaw.

To consolidate power on a post-shame terrain, leaders must be willing to go low. As they go low, progressive politics must be willing to go even lower. We must aim to outrage the outrageous, to out-dada the dadaists. 'Too much!' is a potential rallying cry—too many products, too many choices, too many complacencies, too much of this world!

While postmodernity has been screaming this since May 1968, 2017 has forced us to acknowledge that power has fully co-opted the critique. By way of the commodification of perversification, global capital now rules over an empire of difference that eagerly coordinates a wide arrangement of deviations while also producing many of its own.

Power is now fully diffuse, and the antagonism of Marx's class war has been drowned in an overwhelming sea of difference. This development calls for a reorientation that entails learning how to become contrary—and contrary to contrary. In the case of the no-ology presented here, this contrarian position is the forced choice of 'this not that,' a tearing apart of a system that has become entirely limited, restrictive, and constrained.

Some take their cue from those in the Global South who 'homogenize real differences' to name 'the potential unity of an international opposition, the confluence of anticapitalist countries and forces.'[6] This is a good start. But initiating a progressive politics on a post-truth, post-fact, and more importantly, post-shame terrain also requires the unsightly, and astounding screams of 'no' that occasionally rip apart the grand accords of power.

Though it no-longer demands the total suppression of difference, the immediacy of post-shame capitalism reignites the necessity of the conspiracy of no-ology, the power of the affects of anger and hatred, and the task of destroying worlds if we are to break free from a failed politics of social change dominant since the beginning of the 20th century.

Above all else, this terrain of post-shame has paved a way for a future of necessary destruction—the we-who-scream, in the streets, in the countryside, in the factories, in the offices, in our houses. We, the insubordinate and non-subordinate who say No!, we who say Enough!, enough of your meme games, enough of your banal contradictions, enough of your idiotic playing at soldiers and bosses. We the no-ologists do not want to exploit, who do not have power and do not want to have power, we who want to have lives that we consider humane, we who are without face and without voice—we are the crisis of capitalism.

And it is 2017 we have to thank for the confrontation of this crisis.

locating the alt-right: nick land's romantic irrationalism as critical delirium

As the nascent rise of a populist right in Western Europe and North America has made clear, left-leaning politics have been unable to channel the anti-establishment impulses of the most socio-economically marginalized into a sort of grounded (yet, importantly, non-totalizing) set of ethics, programs, and organizational policies that can proliferate the political vacuum the post-fact terrain has opened up to offer up something appealing in the way of a coherent political program through which to challenge for power.

One cannot help but be dazzled at the speed by which the so-called 'alt-right' mobilized to snatch the support of estranged populations out of the hands of some sort of socially re-oriented left alternative. Plenty of insightful work has been written on the ongoing struggle between left and right to seize the memes of production, but startlingly little has been written (or even asked) about the theoretical origins of this alternative right. Where does it come from? How can we begin to confront it? Perhaps such gaps are due to the fact that the philosophical questions being asked by early trajectories of the alt-right are remarkably similar to those put forward by some forms of speculative, accelerant, and alternative left politics. With the aim of strengthening a critical offensive against the alternative right in mind, this short essay is a trace—an attempt to begin locating the theoretical groundings of the alt-right so we may begin to chip away at its foundations.

Like many stories, this one begins with George Orwell, who popularized the term 'neo-reactionary' in a 1943 essay for Tribune magazine entitled 'As I Please.' Referred to as NRx by its proponents, the neo-reactionary movement favours a return to older societal constructs and forms of government, including support for monarchism and traditional gender roles, coupled with a libertarian, Lockean, or otherwise conservative approach to economics. In a response to the disenfranchisement and increasing inequality wrought by the financial crisis of 2007-08, American computer scientist Curtis Yarvin—writing under the now-infamous nom de plume Mencius Moldbug—articulated many of the tenants later developed into something called 'Dark Enlightenment' thought by English philosopher Nick Land, who first coined the term in a 2012 essay of the same name.

According to Land's essay, the Dark Enlightenment is an ideological analysis of modern democracy that harshly rejects the vision of the 18th century European Enlightenment— a period punctuated by the development of empirical science, the rise of humanist values and the first outburst of revolutionary democratic reform. In contrast to these values, Dark Enlightenment advocates for an autocratic and neo-monarchical society. In the words of Land, its belief system is unapologetically reactionary, feudal even:

"For hardcore neo-reactionaries, democracy is not merely doomed, it is doom itself. Fleeing it approaches an ultimate imperative. Neo-reaction conceives the dynamics of democratization as fundamentally degenerative: systematically consolidating and exacerbating private vices, resentments, and deficiencies until they reach a level of collective criminality and comprehensive social corruption." [1]

While such words are politically illuminating, they reveal little about Land's ontological groundings. For that we need to dig into some of Land's earlier works—works such as The Thirst for Annihilation: Georges Bataille and Virulent Nihilism, published in 1992 when Land was still a lecturer in philosophy at the University of Warwick. Like many theorists that have amassed in the fold of speculative realism, Land's work equips the transcendental materialism of Deleuze and Guattari to probe new possibilities of critical thought engendered by the de-stratification of the Kantian bifurcation —which positions the experience of the transcendental (noumenon) over the empirical (phenomena).

Following from Deleuze, Land turns this critique back upon its presuppositions, in order to affirm a radical immanence in which matter itself is synthetic and productive. So far, most of what we call 'new materialism' echoes Land in arguing that matter is a vibrant, primary process—that everything unfolding at the level of conceptual representation is merely secondary and derivative. Deleuze, for his part, pursues this line through Henri Bergson's critique of representation and the means through which we privilege intuition.

But Land pushes further, initiating a neo-reactionary impetus that scatters the seeds of a virulently alternative anti-humanism by eradicating intuition and everything else that is subjective, phenomenological, or affective. Such an impetus pushes through to romantic irrationalism—what Land calls intensity-in-itself, a thirsting for annihilation via a nihilistic acceleration without ethics. Apart from these frameworks of intuition—frameworks of subjectivity, affect, and phenomenology that Deleuze and Guattari (as well as most other transcendental materialists) are uncomfortable jettisoning entirely—the 'subject' cannot experience intensity, because intensity de-stabilizes/eliminates subjectivity.[2]

This Landian manifestation of transcendental materialism is the pure materialization of critique—one that sets out to first analyze and then undermine systems (philosophical, psychoanalytic, economic, political) with what might be called a 'critical delirium.'[3] By collapsing the hierarchy of the transcendental and empirical, the critique of the Kantian critique of metaphysics is converted into a materialist metaphysics of critique—a reduction of difference to matter Land calls 'the enabling condition for critical philosophy.

However, this incessant eradication of intuition brings Land's speculative realism to an impasse because vitalism is all about having intense experiences. Landianism cannot avail itself of this register of intensification. Land is not interested in phenomenological subjectivity and he's not interested in experiences insofar as they are experiences of a subject in the Deleuzo-Guattarian register—a sort of organism with a face, a personal identity, etc. These are all the things that are supposed to require destratification.

In other words, this speculative project falls precisely because intensification is, for Land: "not translatable into any register of affective experience or affective intensity in exactly the same way that it is not translatable into any register of cognition or conceptualization."[4] For quite some time, those working in affect theory have been claiming that the realm of affect is pre-subjective, and that it includes layers of efficacy and determination that are irreducible to cognition or to concepts. Thus on the one side, the superiority of Land's critical delirium is that his schizophrenic metaphysics confronts the deeply nihilistic consequences of an ethics of intensity, while Deleuze and later affect theorists do not. However, on the flip side, Land has no basis for action besides the one that he has so rigorously destroyed—he wants to maintain that a political project can just keep on intensifying and intensifying without end.

But where is the drive for subjective manipulation? Where is the driving force mobilized to confront the violent onslaught of late capitalism? Ultimately this speculative process of 'death drive' subverts itself. If one's practice is fuelled entirely by the need to always intensify and deterritorialise (without also locating a sort of political subjectivity), there comes a point at which there is no agency left—'you, yourself, and an impetus for social transformation' have dissolved into the process. Inevitably you end up engendering new performative contradictions, and, as Deleuze reminds us, contradictions at the level of concepts manifest themselves as incapacities at the level of practice. In Land's words, such a turn towards romantic irrationalism leads to a kind of 'practical impotence.'

From this practical impotence the route from Land's neo-reactionary speculations to the mutated manifestation of the alt-right—and, relatedly, a fragmented left squabbling over whether historical materialists are too orthodox and new materialists too speculative—is relatively easy to see. For as Land's recent volume of collected writings and/as 'fanged noumena insist on reminding us: "politics must be displaced, it must be deputized, and all you can do is endorse or affirm impersonal processes which at least harbour the promise of generating or ushering in the next phase of deterritorialisation."[5]

For the precarious delirium of Land's romantic irrationality, the only politics left is for the left is fatalistically welcoming the (alt-right) processes that destroy—even in an imagined sense—all critical agencies, capacities, and subjectivities. In practice however, the pure disavowal of any willed praxis essentially results in affirming free markets, deregulation, capitalist desecration of traditional forms of social organization, etc. Put another way, if you have no strategy, someone with a strategy will soon commandeer your tactics. Or as Lacan, responding to Paris protests of May '68, put it: "What you aspire to in initiating an entirely subjectless revolutionary movement is a new master. And you will get one."[6]

Thus Land leads us to a paradigmatic crossroads: the speculative orthodoxy of practical impotence by way of unrelenting and intensifying destratifications and deterritorialisation OR the affective and subject-laden confrontation with the fascistic forces assembling in the gap being left by such vehement death drive. As a postmodern memic manifestation of the right continues to rise in perpetuity, such is the choice we are forced to make.

A position subsumed by the fanged noumena of a perpetually deconstructive nihilism—while productive and inherently transformative in virtual materiality—ends up becoming a pawn of an impersonal, cynical force of libertarian capitalism. A force that celebrates capitalist deterritorialisation for its own sake leads to neo-reaction, neo-feudalism, alt-libertarianism, or whatever else we want to call the emerging politics of Silicon Valley.

The good news: we don't really have to choose between Land's undeniably ingenious destratifications and subjectivity as impetus for social transformation. Once thinking becomes subordinated to an intensifying imperative inherently rejecting representational and epistemological issues, it is clear that there must be a limitrophic point of absolute deterritorialisation towards which the process of affirmation or acceleration tends. If we take matter as nothing but machinic production, self-differentiation, and the fundamental binary that organizes this materialist metaphysics is that between transformative materiality (body without organs) and death (the moment of absolute indifference as absolute difference) then we must ask: Why should critical thought be governed by the imperative to intensify and destratify any more than by the more imperative of self-reflexive representational transformation? If de-stratification and re-presentation are two sides of the same coin should we not fluctuate between the multiple as needed?

on the creation of situations

We devour everything in sight. Primal pleasure lies in the blindly obvious and accessible —the snaffle and grab of desire, a fuel that satisfies us basic creatures for a few hours.

A party is contained, repressed. A party is a wall. It begins and ends, running along an axiom of linearity. It has rules. It charges for cover and for drinks. A party is a commodity. Like an exhaust value slowly re- leasing subversive energies into the ether. A party is a control, a comedy of recognition, an outlet for our de- siring machines to ensure we can consume with consistent vigour come Monday.

In contrast, a situation is turbulent, deranged. A situation is a mirror. It deconstructs a sense of self as independent. It establishes the ego as co-constit-utive, dependent on externality, an other. A situation is a line of flight, a bizarre individualism that explodes out into the endless possibilities of a post-Monday world.

As subjectivity folds in on itself through the phenomenological experience of a situation, this 'other' is elaborated upon within the socio-material frameworks that give subjectivity and its various anxieties its particular characteristics.

The construction of such situations begin beyond the ruins of the modern spectacle. It is easy to see how much the very principle of the spectacle—nonintervention—is linked to the alienation of the world. From pataphysics to the theatre of cruelty, the most pertinent revolutionary experiments in culture have sought to (re)break the spectators' identification with the heroic so as to draw them into activity by provoking their capacities to revolutionise their own lives.Unlike the purely simulative milieu of the party, the situation is designed to be lived by its constructors. It is not a state of exception. The role played by a passive or merely bit-part playing 'public' must be constantly (re)diminished, while that played by those who cannot be called actors, but rather, in a new sense of the term, 'livers,' must steadily and relentlessly be intensified.

We have to multiply poetic subjects and objects—which are now unfortunately so rare that the slightest ones take on an exaggerated emotional importance—and we have to organize partisan games for these poetic subjects to play with these poetic objects. This entire program is essentially transitory. As opposed to the party, the situation is ephemeral, it is without a future. Passageways. Speculative Time Complexes. Our only concern is with performance, real life—we must care nothing about the permanence of art or of anything else.

To create a situation is to present a revolutionary alternative to the ruling culture—not so as to imitate the bourgeois aesthetes who try to restrict people to what has already been done. What has already been done shouldn't bother us. We must know that creation is never pure—it is destructive, fragmenting, an orgy of adultered hallucination.

70

a postcard from the frontlines of late capitalism

backyard reading and cigar smoking
fuck backyards
fuck cigars.

how to you type if there is no typewriter font?
do you even type bro?
do you even hype bro?

look out for the hype machine and your favourite prom queen
were you valedictorian?
the most popular social historian?

blazing trails in a souped-up delorian,
arthur cravan at the wheel drunk on singapore slings and morphine that we got over the counter at a library in mexico city.

'umour, a theatrical uselessness without joy, a uselessness of everything.
amour, the same, except with sprinkles of amour fati.
now give me incessant meaningless activity as an expression of futility
or give me de-nihilism to its extreme of death
it doesn't matter which, obviously.

keep your progress,
your regressive platitudes,
your smug banalities of violent machinic individualism.

send me your letters de guerre,
your postcard from the frontlines of late capitalism
trenches, they overflow with thick viscous pools of
depression.

we're told that anxiety is a self-imposed death-sentence
a decade hence, as the only life raft.
a magnetic field of uncultivated poppies
where pierre janet and jonbenét take opium tea with
fourteen lumps, not two.

schizo-autonomism,
poetic anonymity as we take turns playing the exquisite
corpse
where we slack off work,
as poetry is made by all, not one.

thus spoke the comte de lautreamont,
thus spoke the paper bag full of airplane motion sickness.

we have no talent,
we are merely modest copying machines of molecular
manifestos
vestigial subjects hallucinating vividly from visceral
hunger.

a journey into the non-conscious beast of affective
verisimilitude,
which places the spirit of revolt far above politics,
and once again, the french call it priest eating.

we the affectariat

"Inspiring sad passions is necessary for the exercise of power. Rulers need the sadness of their subjects." — Whispered in a bar in Cannes by Gilles Deleuze in the late 1970s.

We love questions of who and how. Who is the agent of history? How will social transformation come about?

The proletariat occupied the position it did in classical Marxism not because of some metaphysical virtù, but because Marxists believed industrial workers occupied a position in society that equipped them to transform it and thereby lead other social elements in doing so.

This position faltered over the course of the mid-twentieth century economic boom, where many of us came to see the labour movement as quite complacently situated on the terrain of power rather than leading social change.

The ongoing co-optation of social movements organized at the intersections of capital's violence (gender, race, class) cast a concept of agency—premised on the overcoming of alienation and the emergence of the authentic self—into question. And with this authentic self goes the whole imaginary edifice of collective social transformation.

Agency and structure are co-constitutive. And now all we are left with is a humanistic pessimism—an insufficient force of social transformation.

The Oedipal foundations of society, despite these impressive shakings given by various social movements, stands firm, and is perhaps even strengthened.

Gone is the individual self— the former site and agent of our liberation. Gone is the unshakable belief in some majestic dialectical un- folding of our closed, repressed human freedoms.

Flows of desire, the operations of social machinery—all along these have preceded and determined the 'reasoning individual.'

The sense of a self capable of political agency had given many of us an entry point into political action.

The loss of individual agency threatens to close off our only known route to some sort of struggle for freedom. It replaces dreams of emancipation with nightmares of the little man—the fascist in us all, in our heads, in our hearts, in our everyday behaviours, it is this micro-fascism which causes us to desire power, to long for the very thing that dominates us and exploits us.

Affect offers a new approach to this old problem.

What latent thing do you and I, two utterly powerless, simulated individuals, share that might, if activated in some way, endow us with a common sense of things, and from there a collective potency?

Viscerality is not some sort of authentic self buried by oppression—it constructs something new in the wreckage of defeat. It assembles collectivity's against the fascist on your shoulder that whispers: "You are totally alone in this—in this dead-end job, this broken home, this bottomless debt, this paralyzing depression."

We must work to embolden the visceral potency of the othered—women, people of colour, and all of those for whom political defeat means confronting the unknowable face of human catastrophe.

The consignment of billions of people to poverty and precarity, the roll-back of basic victories like the right to birth control and abortion, the criminalisation and incarceration of millions of people of colour, and the utter evisceration of the age-old social supports on which the poor and working class have depended for survival.

In times such as these, sadness is no longer acceptable an an adequate response.

Sadness is easy—it is the affect of impotence, a precarious position that most marginalized at the folds of gender, race, and class cannot afford to hold.

As it points towards action, anger is much harder. But that is what we must draw upon now. We must become an collectively visceral anger that will no longer allow itself to be satisfied with desiring its own repression any more.

high anxiety: capitalism and schizoanalysis

There is an emergent disconnection between the focuses of activism and the current structure of oppression in everyday life. What revolutionary politics lacks is a new psychology, an anti-psychiatry that will help us to undertake the task of gradually releasing our repressed emotional, visceral, and affective concerns from the grips of our current society continuous of control.[1] The primary aim of schizoanalysis is to fulfill this lack — to take the affirmative possibilities of contemporary groundlessness to its limits in order to rupture the anxious realities of neoliberal capitalism (realities such as the NSA, CCTV, performance management reviews, the unemployment office, the privileges system in the prisons, Trump's presidential victory, the constant examination and classification of young schoolchildren). Indeed, to push through the limits imposed by the psychological alienation of capitalism, to replace our position as Oedipualized, defenseless, guilt-ridden puppets in internal straight-jackets, with free, empowered, de-securitized, uncoded subjects that have the tools to overcome anxiety by transforming fear into anger, and acting on this anger through affective projectiles of attack.[2]

Etymologically, the schiz in schizophrenia and schizoanalysis comes from skhizein, which means to split, break, separate, rupture, or divide. With schizophrenia, this refers to the 'split' in the mind, or the multiple, broken up experiences of someone with schizophrenia.[3] Schizoanalysis operates by extracting the emancipatory potential of the schiz — the ability to constantly break free from the dominant emotional controls — from the debilitating disorientations of the illness in order to locate exactly where and how these breaks in reality arise in the social, and then mobilize them to manufacture new forms of affective resistances.

According to the French theorists Gilles Deleuze and Felix Guattari, who coined the term, schizoanalysis is not a political ideology; it is an active, creative force that works micro-politically from the bottom up to raise radical political consciousnesses by uprooting people from the reactive social causes and traditions that have placed them in a state of perpetual anxiety. Deleuze and Guattari contrast this active force of schizoanalysis with the reactive force of capital-induced anxiety — a process of alienation and decomposition that disempowers and segments populations by turning them against each other and themselves by making social spaces "neat and orderly," creating governable subjects conducive to top-down quantification and control, and providing the work-discipline and speed which capitalism demands. In other words, the reactive forces of capitalism create anxiety through bodily, emotional and sexual repression that operates through a restriction, a blockage, and a redirection of affect.

Anxiety within capitalism is reactive and personalized: from New Right discourses blaming the poor for poverty, to contemporary therapies which treat anxiety as a neurological imbalance or a dysfunctional thinking style, a hundred varieties of management discourse — time management, anger management, parental management, self-branding, and gamification — all offer anxious subjects an illusion of control in return for ever-greater conformity to the capitalist model of subjectivity. By complicating these doctrines of individual responsibility which reinforce vulnerability and disposability, schizoanalysis offers us a creative way to confront these anxieties plaguing contemporary politics in the Global North.[4]

Take a survey the current political landscape. During his annexation of Crimea, Vladimir Putin appeared on national television and avowed that there were no Russian soldiers in Ukraine. With spectacular conviction, Donald Trump took center stage at a rally and insisted that the Mexican government wittingly allows "bad" immigrants to cross the US–Mexico border. In somber fashion, Boris Johnson proclaimed the Brexit campaign was bravely staring down a direct threat of Germano-Franco-European military intervention.

What is so different about the likes of Putin, Trump, and Johnson? After all, ideologues have never been the type to let contradictory facts get in the way of a rousing speech. But these men aren't lying so much as signaling, with unabashed arrogance, that the truth doesn't matter anymore, that we are living in a "post-fact" or "post-truth" world: not merely a world in which politicians and media lie (they have always lied to secure power), but one in which they are no longer forced to appeal to facts or address their critics in order to be successful.

Technology is often blamed for such a reductio ad absurdum. If a lie is clickable, it will feed into existing prejudices. This is the nature of a networked society. Supraliminal algorithms curated by Facebook and Google are now based largely on our previous search histories. Social media, now the primary news source for most of the connected world, have pushed us deeper into an echo chamber of interpretation, wherein every version of an event is just another narrative and lies can be excused as an alternative point of view or an opinion, because it's all relative and everyone has her own truth.

Yet social media platforms are merely a means through which a post-fact world is being distributed. This desire to take shelter in a personal techno-fantasy is a symptom tethered firmly to an underlying economic, social, and political anxiety which has manifested as an impending sense of uncertainty that has spread from the individuals into the whole of the social field.

After all, if the empirical data — what we call "the facts" — say "you have no economic future," "the environment is deteriorating at an unprecedented rate," and traditional sources of "stability and security" such as the state and market are culpable in all of it, why would you want to hear facts? If you live in a world where political instability in Central Asia leads to the loss of livelihoods in Detroit, where governments seem to have no control over what is going on, public trust in the institutions of authority — politicians, academics, the media — buckles under the weight of our collective uncertainties. Anxiety is a pandemic of postmodernity.[5]

From the 2011 dismantling of the Occupy encampments in Zuccotti Park to the recent dispersion of Black Lives Matter protests in Dallas, the inability of contemporary social movements to develop viable, long-term alternatives to the destabilizing processes of capitalism is directly related to their failure to respond to the reactive problem of anxiety. In actively confronting the condition of collective anxieties, schizoanalysis offers an alternative basis for a political project which provokes a new way of resisting the rhetoric, fear, control, and perpetual uncertainty that characterizes the groundlessness of our post-fact era.

By rejecting the internal attribution of blame and the individual orientation of therapy, schizoanalysis emphases social oppression and collective responses. This perspective can transform the anger and alienation resulting from the oppressive experiences of capitalism into a more positive, focused kind of discontent. In situating the problem of anxiety socially (as opposed to individually), schizoanalysis affords us the creativity to feel anger, both as subjects and a collectivity, which can overcome earlier prohibitions by making anger an energizing force for change, increasing confidence, and enhancing activist relations.

By analyzing the ways in which the "personal is political," activists can overcome the reactive personalization of oppression and begin to see the ways in which each phase of capitalism is qualified by a particular affect — emotion, way of relating, bodily disposition — that holds it together.[6] This is not a static situation. As capitalism is always redefining its own limits, it constantly comes into crisis and recomposes and reterritorializes around new affects. As its power comes largely from its alienating force, the pervasiveness of a particular form of affect management only lasts until strategies of resistance break down its social source.

An international organization of revolutionary artists, activists and theorists known as the Situationists emphasize that every phase of affect management under capitalism is a public secret: something that, though everyone knows and experiences, nobody publicly acknowledges or talks about. As long as the dominant affect of anxiety is a public secret, it remains effective, and strategies directed against its sources cannot emerge.

Thinking of capitalism as a mode of managing our dominant affects presents an alternative to theories that celebrate the rise of immaterial labor — labor that produces informational and cultural content as commodities — as a path to eventual liberation through the unleashing of human creative power. Theories of immaterial labor wrongly assume that capitalism releases human creative potential and that the main problem is merely the privatization of its product. In other words, they locate the problem not in the processes of capitalism itself, but rather in the ways in which it commodifies outputs.

If capitalism is conceived of as a mode of affect management it clearly does not release human creativity in new forms so much as it reactively traps them in anxiety through a compulsion to communicate in terms of artificial social performances grounded in the dominant system's terms. Simply put, alienation is internal to the functioning logics of post-fact capitalism, not merely the exploitation of its production. For example, the dominant narrative suggests we need more stress so as to keep us "safe" (through securitization) and "competitive" (through performance management). Each moral panic, crackdown or new round of repressive laws, adds to the cumulative weight of anxiety and stress arising from general over-regulation. Real, human insecurity is channeled into fuelling securitization. This is a vicious circle, because securitization increases the very alienation (surveillance, regulation) which causes the initial anxieties.

Illustrative of this alienation are the ways in which capitalism reinforces vulnerability and disposability. It keeps people fragmented and disillusioned by personalizing responsibility for collective crises like rampant inequality and global warming. Instead of being urged to confront the sources of these social ills — the fiscal servitude imposed on the Global South by outrageous IMF loans or a steadfast commitment to expanding fossil fuel capacities, for example — citizens of developed-world nations are told to keep calm, donate to charity, participate in patronizing "voluntourism" projects, recycle, refrain from watering the lawn on weekdays, and compost kitchen scraps. All of this is further reinforced by a self-esteem industry that tells people how to achieve success through positive thinking, as if the sources of anxiety and frustration are simply illusory. Philanthropy, therapy, and the self-esteem industry exemplify the way in which problems that are directly related to social reproduction are re-framed in terms of individual psychology.

In a similar way, public secrets are typically individualized. The problem of anxiety — that familiar, unpleasant rumination informing psychosomatic turmoil — is only visible at the personal, psychological level, its social causes remain concealed. In other words, each phase of capitalism blames the system's victims for the suffering that the system causes. As a result, capitalism vindicates its own violences by portraying the fundamental part of its functional logic as a contingent and localized problem: in the same way capitalism faults the poor for their poverty, it blames the depressed for their anxiety.

Of course, anxiety is not new under capitalism. As early as the 1930s, psychoanalyst William Reich theorized anxiety as the result of a conflict between the libido — unconscious desire — and the outer world. What is new about capital's management of affect in a post-fact era is that anxiety now subsumes the whole of the social and emotional field, rather than being concentrated in specific spaces such as sexuality.[7]

There are various mechanisms for this total subsumption of anxiety. Professionalized networking permits communication only along systemically mediated paths; existence becomes reduced to 140 characters or less, and that which cannot be communicated within this limit is systematically excluded. The internalization of these mechanisms leads to self-surveillance and self-association with quality metrics and social media networks. French theorist Paul Virilio refers to this phenomenon as "telepresence," or the immediate presence of different spaces to one another. Telepresence causes generalized vulnerability to the gaze of others. The result is a culture of groundless reconsumption underpinned entirely by anxious social performances that, rather than producing sites of creativity and empowerment, compel people to keep up the appearance of simulated happiness and participation in order to maintain their followers.

During periods of mobilization such as May 1968 — a state of unrest characterized by demonstrations, massive general strikes, and the occupation of universities and factories that started in France and spread across Europe — people felt a sense of empowerment, the ability to actively express themselves, a sense of authenticity and de-repression or de-alienation that can act as an effective treatment for psychosomatic despondency. A kind of affective plateau, the opening of previously unimaginable political possibilities, however impermanent, is what is needed in order to rejuvenate activism over the long-term.

In their work on power, resistance and conflict, social movement theorists Athina Karatzogianni and Andrew Robinson refer to this moment as the click, that is, the moment in which societal inequities are realized. It is the instant at which experiences and feelings suddenly make sense in relation to the repressive bureaucracies of capitalism — something quite different from conceptualizing structural violence in the abstract. Afterwards participants feel that they know the impact of affect management, that they have an affective answer to the "why?" of resistance. This is crucial for an emotional transformation of anger and fear towards a sense of injustice, a type of empowered anger which is less resentful and more focused, a move towards self-expression, and a reactivation of resistance. "The click" brings about validation and focus to our anxiety, a focus which is different from the hopelessness and frustration experienced previously in that it exercises voice, it moves the reference of truth and reality from the system to the speaker, contributing to the reversal of perspective – seeing the world through one's positions and desires, rather than the system's.

Such experiences have become much rarer in recent years. Anxious individuals are faced with immense difficulties in acknowledging their reality and pain in a world in which something must be counted by "quality" regimes or mediated by television or the Internet to be validated as real. Many of them are unaware of the fact that they belong to an oppressed group because the repressive bureaucracies of the society of control have become normalized and their psychological effects personalized. The unacknowledged nature of anxiety as a public secret within dominant political, economic, and social discourses further reiterates this point.

. . .

Social movements today do not have the proper mechanisms in place for combating anxiety. Calls for deliberate exposure to high-anxiety situations — physical confrontations with the police, open marches in the streets — are indicative of the reactionary indisposition of contemporary social movements towards anxiety. For example, a traditional tactic, what activists call the "do-ology," is that of the vague injunction, "Just stop being afraid!" Yet anxiety is not simply the specter haunting action; it is a material force — the psychoanalytic apparatuses of control are very much material, and thus the question of overcoming the specters of anxiety is rarely as simple as consciously rejecting it.

The intensified securitization of the surveillance state makes this process of recognition and resistance even more difficult as affect management takes on the form of preemptive control techniques that stop protests before they start or before they can achieve anything. Kettling, mass detainments, stop-and-search, lockdowns, preemptive arrests, group infiltrations, and practices of disposability, such as violent dawn raids and unmitigated police brutality, are examples of these kinds of tactics.

What's more, psychosomatic torture techniques — "punishment by process," as French theorist Michel Foucault terms them — keep individuals fearful and feeling vulnerable through the abuse of procedures designed for other purposes, such as keeping people on pre-charge or pre-trial bail conditions in order to disrupt their everyday activities, using no-fly and border-stop lists to harass known dissidents, needlessly putting people's photographs in the press, arresting people on suspicion, using pain-compliance holds, or quietly making known that someone is under surveillance. While fear of state interference has been a tactic of control for centuries, today such tactics are inflated and reinforced by an ever-expanding web of visible surveillance gridded across public space which act as strategically placed triggers of trauma and anxiety.

Needed now are not just better tactics for confronting preemptive control or circumventing psychosomatic torture. Rather, needed are long-term strategies for disrupting this lynchpin of subordination. Needed is a machine for combatting anxiety. This is something which does not yet exist, because what the Situationists call a reversal of perspective has yet to be accomplished. Today's main forms of resistance are largely ineffective precisely because they are based in struggles against previous forms of more overtly physical repression.

Most of the strategies employed by current social movements tend to mirror what has worked in the past. Strikes, wage struggles, co-operatives, partisan political alternatives, street protests, the refusal to work, working to rule, and occupying various public spaces may have proven highly effective in combating earlier manifestations of state repression, but they are largely ignorant to the ways power is modularized today.

Take Occupy's attempts at capturing Zuccotti Park and other public spaces. Occupy failed in its actions, and its anti-corporate messages were subsequently coopted by the partisan power of Democratic presidential candidate Senator Bernie Sanders. Its failure owed in large part to the rise of the surveillance state. Public spaces where people can engage in free speech and assembly unobstructed by state and corporate power don't exist anymore.

When Black Lives Matter occupied a Minneapolis police station, their every movement was surveilled and recorded 24/7 by a dozen adjacent security cameras. When rioters in London took to occupying their neighbourhood streets and shops to protest the police shooting of Mark Duggan in 2011, the state stood aside, let the riots run their course, and then proceeded to round up over 5000 people by cross-referencing their actions with thousands of hours of CCTV footage. And when a pro-Palestinian demonstration broke out in Toronto in 2012, police were able to intercept and shutdown the march by following the detailed instructions posted by organizers on various social media sites.

What has self-securitized actions such as these is the gap between radical processes of thought and traditional practices of action. Simply put, though Occupy and similar movements have illuminated the ways capitalism is deployed as power for violating populations according to dominant socio-material logics controlled by white, wealthy, masculine, minoritarian (a minority that wields an over representative degree of political control) groups, their

80

mobilizations take place on a plane of traditional tactics. They protest, march, and occupy, all strategies which have been proven ineffective in our securitized climate.

This situation creates a feeling of powerlessness, when people are not in fact powerless. In Precarious Rhapsody (2009) Italian theorist Franco Berardi points to how unemployed youths suggest they are often hopeless both about getting work and rebelling — the desire for "something more" has been corroded.

We must re-direct our energies towards creating active configurations of sufficient power for interrupting the dominant construction of anxiety; a reversal of perspective, a unifying break, a click, a moment in which it is realized that tactics must be immanent to thought. And while more traditional tactics can and still work effectively against more traditional forms of repression, a politics of schizoanalysis pushes us to directly confront our anxieties by learning that it is good and positive to express our viscerality, to be angry and to convey anger every time we confront the affect management of capitalism.

Such a visceral emancipation is crucial in transforming our anxiety into active forces which enable recomposition, such as love, courage, laughter and focused anger. As a result, the consciousness–raising processes of schizoanalysis are psychologically positive in untying knots and releasing active force because they allow for a recognition of anxiety as a social effect and a matter of power, which can in turn, shift perceptions of the social field from a game of competitive success to a conflict scenario and a narrative of oppression and liberation. In other words, the central contribution of schizoanalysis is the discovery that modern (reactive) anxiety and its resultant feelings of powerlessness actually contain (active) resistance to capitalism.

By extracting the emancipatory potential of the schiz — the ability to constantly break free from the dominant forms of emotional control — a schizoanalytical perspective offers a contingent grounding for an anxious, groundless world — a way of deepening our understanding of the post-fact society by pointing to the ways in which the transformation of reactive affects into movement-focused anger and courage is only viable through the reconfigurations of horizontal connections that stave off both meaninglessness and isolation.

Such schizoanalytical reconfigurations require:

1. the production of new non-dogmatic theories relating to experience (our own perceptions of our situation are blocked or

cramped by dominant assumptions, and need to be made explicit);

2. recognising the reality, and the systemic nature, of our experiences (we need to affirm that our pain is really pain, that what we see and feel is real, and that our problems are not only personal);

3. the transformation of emotions (people are paralyzed by unnameable emotions that need to be transformed into a sense of injustice);

4. creating expressive voice (the exercise of voice moves the reference of truth and reality from the system to the speaker, contributing to the reversal of perspective – seeing the world through one's own perspective and desires, rather than the system's).

The point is not simply to recount experiences but to transform and restructure them through their theorization. Participants change the dominant meaning of their experience by mapping it with different assumptions. This is often done by finding patterns in experiences which alleviates anxiety by providing political awareness of the origins of affects while simultaneously gesturing towards the power of group support. Seeing personal problems and small injustices as symptoms of wider structural problems has the power to initiate the "frightening" (active) as opposed to the "frightened" (reactive).

Social movements are only a frightening force when they do not succumb to anxiety. Moving forward, we must work toward providing an alternative to processes that begin and end with the development of critical capacities, as well as to approaches that funnel critical development into traditional organizations. By reconnecting with our experiences now — rather than theories from past forms of affect management — recognizing the shared, systemic nature of our experiences, and working to transform emotions and construct dis-alienating spaces by unifying through patterns in our shared experiences, a politics of schizoanalysis is an anti-psychiatric form of collective care that has the potential to mutate into affinity groups within a wide network of autonomous organizations that have the critical and tactical capacities to move beyond reactive critique and towards active social transformation.

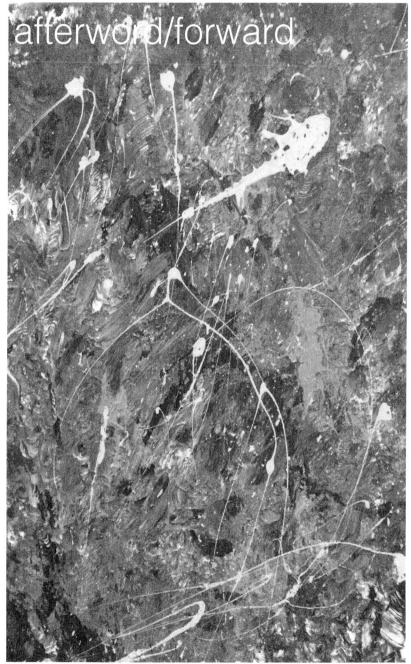

afterword/forward

integrated world capitalism and molecular revolution*

This text was presented by Felix Guattari at the Conference on Information and/as New Spaces of Liberty (CINEL), which took place in Rio de Janeiro in the Fall of 1981. It has been translated into English—for the first time ever in print—by the author.

Integrated World Capitalism (IWC) does not respect existing territorialities, nor traditional ways of life, nor the social organization of our national assemblies—all of which appear more established than ever before in representational history.

Contemporary capitalism can be defined as integrated world capitalism be-cause it has already settled all surfaces on the planet. No human activity can escape its grasp as it works to further over-code and control every mode of socio-political expression.

This double extension of geography—a movement that closes in on itself and a molecular proliferative expansion—is correlative of a general process of deterritorialization.[1] While the social organization of national assemblies appear more established than ever before, IWC does not respect existing territorialities nor the traditional ways of life. It recon-structs production systems and social systems on its own foundations, on what I call its own axiomatic (axiomatic being opposed here to programmatic).

In other words, IWC is not program defined once and for all: it is about a crisis, an un-expected difficulty that adds and subtracts additional functional axioms. Some capitalist forms seem to collapse during a world war or a crisis like that of 1929, but then they are reborn in other forms, they find other grounds. This deterritorialization and permanent recomposition concerns both power formations[2] and modes of production (I prefer to talk about power formations rather than modes of production, as this notion is too restrictive of the subject considered here).

84

Here I will address the issue of IWC from three vital perspectives:

- That of its production systems, of its economic expression and the of IWC's axiomatization of Socius;[3]
- The segmentations it has developed at the transnational level, in the European Union, and at the molecular level;
- Finally, in terms of what I refer to as the revolutionary war machines,[4] the fittings of desire,[5] and class struggles.

iwc and its production systems

It is important to remember that there is more than just an international division of labour —there is a globalization of the division of labor that generally captures all modes of activities, including those form-ally beyond the economic definition of work. Even the most 'backward' industries and marginal production methods, domestic activities, sports, and cultures, which managed to circumvent the world market, are falling, one after another, into a rapids of territoralisation.

IWC thus incorporates all of our machinic systems,[6] human labours and all other kinds of social and institutional spaces—such as technical and scientific arrangements, public facilities, or the media. The computer revolution is greatly accelerating this integration process, which also contaminates in the un-conscious subjectivity of both the individual and social. As it is constitutive of the production process, this machinic semiotic integration[7] of human labor works to model each worker not only by what they know— what some economists call 'knowledge capital'—but also by all its systems of inter-action with human society and the machinic environment.

the economic expression of iwc

The economic expression of IWC—its subjugating semiotics, which fashion both people and communities—is not merely a monetary system of signs, scholars or legal devices related to wage, property, and public order. It also relies on systems of servitude[8] in a cybernetic sense. Semi-otic components of capital always operate on two registers: that of representation (where the sign systems are independent and distanced economic referents) and that of diagrammatic (where the sign systems come directly into concatenation[9] with referents as modelling tools, programming, planed social segments, and productive arrangements).

Thus, capital is much more than a simple economic category relating to the circulation and accumulation of goods. It is a semiotic category that affects all levels of production and all levels of the stratification of power. IWC registers not only in the context of societies divided in to social classes, racial, bureaucratic, sex and age groups, but also within the tissues of our machinic proliferation. Its ambiguity with regard to material and semi-otic machinic mutations characteristic of the present situation is such that it uses all the machinic power and semiotic proliferation of developed industrial societies. At the same time its power is masked by means of specific economic expression. It promotes innovation and machinic expansion which it can later recover and consolidate into fundamental social axioms on which it will not compromise: an en-coded type of social arrangement, desire, work, leisure, and culture.

the axiomisation of the socius

In the current context, the axiomatization of Socius is characterized by three types of processing: closure, deterritorialization, and the general system of segmentarity—the complex interrelations between all of which will be explored here in detail.

i. closure

From the moment when capitalism invaded all economically exploitable surfaces, it could no longer maintain the expansioary impetus that was possible during its colonial and imperialist phases. As a result, its limits are now contained, which requires capitalism to recompose endlessly around itself—around the same spaces, deepening its modes of control and its subjugation of human societies. Far from being a growth factor, capital-ism's globalization corresponds to a rad-ical rethinking of previous bases. It can lead either to a complete involution of the system, or a radical transfer of power. IWC finds its expansion, its growth, work-ing within the same formations of power, reconverting social relationships, and developing ever more artificial markets, not only in the field of goods but also in affect. I hypothesize that the current crisis—which in reality is not one, but rather multiplicitious convergences of crises—is this oscillation between the involution of a certain type of capitalism that directly faces its own fence, and a restructuring attempt from different bases.

ii. deterritorialization

IWC must, in other words, facilitate a decisive conversion that completely liquidates earlier systems of social organization—whether at the level of product-ion or the level of national compromise (with bourgeois democracies or social democracies).

This is the end of capitalist territoriality and its expansive imperialism and the shift towards a new form of intensive and deterritorialized imperialism—this abandonment of a number of social categories, branches of activities, and areas over which IWC was based is made possible by the remodeling and taming of the productive forces of the Socius so that they adapt to the new mode of deterritorialized production.

The deterritorialization of capital itself is what Marx has already called the "expropriation of the bourgeoisie by the bourgeoisie," but this time, it is on a different scale. After all, IWC is not necessarily a

86

universalizing force. It does not render bourgeois democracies through-out the world, nor does it forcefully instil dictatorship systems. What it needs is not a flattened political terrain, but a standardization of production patterns, traffic patterns, and social control modes. It is this unique concern that has led IWC to rely on relatively democratic regimes while, simultaneously, imposing dictator-ships. In general, this orientation has the effect of disregarding the old social and political territoriality, or, at the very least, of divesting from their economic powers. But this is possible only if capital itself works to a multiply its own decision centers. Today, IWC has no single center of power. Even its North American branch is polycentric. The actual decision-making centers are spread across the globe. It is not only economic staff at the top—there are various workings of power at all levels of the social pyramid, from the manager to the father (Oedipus). IWC creates its own internal democracy. It does not necessarily require a decision along the lines of its immediate interests. By complex mechanisms, it 'consults' other interests, other segments with which it must deal. This policy of 'negotiation' is different from previous arrangements. It involves information systems and psychological manipulations on an imaginably large scale through the mass media.

The degeneration of concentric modes and hierarchies of power that were level-led in stages from the aristocracy down to the proletariat— mediated by the petit bourgeoisie—is not incompatible with these partial classifications. However, such hierarchies no longer correspond to actual fields of decision making. IWC power is always elsewhere, it is the heart of the mechanisms of deterritorialization. This is what makes it seem impossible to define, reach, and confront it. Moreover, such deterritorializing processes also create paradoxical phenomena —regions of massive underdevelopment within the most developed countries and, conversely, the appearance of hyper-capitalized urban centers (i.e. Dubai, Macau, Doha) within underdeveloped countries.

iii. general system of segmentarity

At the geopolitical level, capitalism is no longer in a phase of expansion. Rather, it is moving to reinvent itself in the same spaces through the technique of palimpsest.[10] As either a center or/and a periphery of the system, capitalism cannot grow any more—its axioms are already hyper-saturated—and thus it turns and re-turns synchronously. For IWC, the problem is in finding new methods of consolidating its systems of social hierarchy. This is its fundamental axiom—to maintain the consistency of the collective forces working across the planet, IWC is required to coexist in areas of hyper-development and hyper-enrichment for the benefit of capitalist aristocracies (who are no longer localized in traditional capitalist bastions), as well as areas of relative underdevelopment and even areas of absolute impoverishment.

Between these extremes is a general disciplining of collective hard work and a partition—the establishment of spaces of global segmentarisation. The free movement of goods and people is now reserved exclusively for the new aristocracies of capitalism. All other categories of people are assigned to residences at the corners of the planet, which have become a truly global factory complete with forced labor or death camps that can span entire countries.

This constant redefinition of social segments is not only about economic power—it is the whole of social life being remodeled. In Eastern France for example, I (Guattari) lived with my father off the steel, until IWC decided to liquid-ate the industrial landscape. Many other spaces such as this one will be trans-formed into tourist areas or residential areas for the elite. Planes of new luxury continue to be erected at the cost of entire regions. New interactions and new antagonisms arise between the segments of IWC and the human arrangements that seek to resist its axiomatic through less marginalizing bases.

Under what conditions it is worthwhile to continue living in such a system? What are these unconscious ties that force us to continue to adhere to such injustices in spite of ourselves? All these segmentarity axioms are bonded to each other. IWC not only intervenes in the world, it also penetrates us at the most most personal level—unconscious molecular determinations that continue to interact with key components of the IWC with an unprecedented and unexplored invasiveness.

transnational segmentarity

The North-South confrontation tends to lose its consistency. Even during phases of intensity like the one, which has persisted for some time, we have taken a turn towards the artificial, the theatrical. Because most of the contradictions are no longer situated in the North-South axis, but in the self-other axis—with the understanding that it is always, ultimately, for IWC to ensure control of all areas that tend to escape, and that there are self and other within each country.

It is enough, then, I think, to say that the new segmentarity sits at the 'cross' between a critical phenomenon—a latent, implicit war between self and other—as well as a secondary phenomenon, an explicit rival-ry between North and South.

The cleavage of the de-development of the South (even within the super-trading oil countries of the Middle East) has created an absolute-path-of-poverty—a process of extermination which has become a permanent feature of the current situation. But other factors also come into play.

The opposition between transnational capitalism, multinational/international lobbies, and national capitalism, while retaining local importance, is not really re-levant from a global point of view. In fact, all these international contradictions organize themselves, meet, and develop complex combinations that cannot be reduced in North-South, self-other, or national-multinational axiomatics. They proliferate as a kind of rhizome,[11] a multi-dimensional assemblage that includes countless historical, religious, and geo-political peculiarities. One can not over-emphasize the fact that the axiomatization—the production of new axioms in response to these specific situations—is not part of a general program, nor de-pendent on a central executive that directs such axioms. The axiomatic of IWC is not based on ideological analyses, it is part of the process of production.

In such a context, any prospect of revolutionary struggle confined to domestic spaces, as well as any prospect of taking political power by way of the dictatorship of the proletariat, appear increasingly illusory. Projects of social transformation are doomed to impotence if they do not engage in a subversive strategy at the global register.

the european segmentarity

The opposition in Europe between North and South is bound to change significantly in the coming years. What appeared to be a fundamental antagonism will per-haps prove to be increasingly 'phago-cytable'—i.e. negotiable at all levels. So no Sino-American model, no return to a pre-war proto-fascism, but rather an evolution, by successive approximations, to-wards an authoritarian system of 'democracy' in a new form.

The methods of repression and social control of Northern and Southern actors tend to approach one other—a perman-ent zone of securitization from the Urals to the Mediterranean threatens to relay the current European judicial agenda.

molecular segmentarity

In capital-intensive areas, we constantly find two types of basic problems:

- Struggles, in the more classical sense, for economic, social, and trade union interests;
- Struggles, which I will group in the register of the molecular revolution, for desire, for freedom, for an environment in which to question everyday life.

The struggles for interest—questions regarding the general standard of living—remain carriers of essential contradictions. We must not underestimate their importance. Yet one can assume that, due to the fact that such struggles lack a comprehensive strategy, they serve primarily as a process through which revolutionary energies are re-integrated into the axiomatic of IWC. They can never lead themselves towards a real social trans-formation. They can never move us towards direct confrontations such as the Paris Commune of 1848 or the Bolshevik Revolution of 1917—they simply do not offer a clear break of class against class necessary to initiate the redefinition of a new type of society. In case of force majeure event, IWC is able to trigger a kind of international ORSEC strategy,[12] a sort of permanent Marshall Plan.

European countries, Japan and the United States can collectively subsidize loss, and for a long time, maintain capitalism as a bastion of powerful market fluctuations. At stake is the survival of IWC, which functions here as a kind of international insurance company that has in reserve enough financialized capital to weather even the most difficult storms.

So what will happen? Will the current crisis lead to a new social status quo of standardization, marginalization and ghettoization—a generalized welfare State with an oversaturated media machine that offers but a few niches of freedom here and there? It is a possibility but it's not the only one.

As soon as we move beyond simplistic patterns, we see that countries like Germany and Japan are not immune to major social upheavals. At least in France anyways, it seems that the situation is evolving towards a liquidation of the sociological balance which manifested itself for decades by way of a relative parity between the left and right forces. We are moving towards a fundamental shifting of the terrain—a new deterritorialization in which over half of the populous—frightened and dazed by the mass media—huddle into a conservative culling (i.e. Trump 2016), while a seizable minority remains more or less refractory.

But if we approach this problem from another angle, not only from struggles of interest, but from molecular struggles, then the panorama changes. What appears in these social spaces—spaces in which systems of control are working intensively to square and sanitize—is a kind of social bacteriological war, some-thing that no longer stays within clearly defined fronts—gendered, racialized, and class fronts—but as molecular changes that are difficult to comprehend. Multi-faceted viruses of this kind are already addressing the social body in its relation-ship to consumption, work, recreation and culture (autodidactions that disseminate like free radios to question the work of the political representation system).

Mutations of unpredictable consequences have began to emerge within subjectivity—modulated through consciousness and the unconscious such mutations are already operating within (in) dividuals and social groups.

assemblages, desire, class struggle
How far can we go this molecular revolution? Is it not doomed, in the best case, to vacillate in the ghettos of South-Other? Would the molecular sabotage of dominant social subjectivities take us far enough? Should this molecular revolution spend its

reserve of emancipatory social forces on engaging in struggles for mere interest at the molar level?

The main thesis supported here is that the axioms of IWC—closure, deterritorialization, and new segmentarites—will never be able to deal with the molecular sabotage of dominant social subjectivities. The resources of IWC may be limit-less in regards to the production and manipulation of institutions and laws. But they face, and will face (ever more violently), a real wall—a maze of impassable confrontations introduced by a libidinal economy[13] which posits that the molecular revolution is not just about everyday relations between men, women, gays, straights, children, and adults in all categories.

After all, the libidinal economy functions first and foremost as a flow of producing-mutation. It reveals the soft underbelly of the mental processes involved in a new global division of labor rendered by the technological revolution.

This does not mean that the molecular revolution automatically brings forth a social revolution that is capable of giving birth to a society, economy and culture that provides an alternative to IWC. After all, was it not a molecular revolution driven by desire which served to pave the way for National Socialism's rise to pow-er? It is important to remember that when a molecular revolution opens the flows of desires it is a wholly undetermined open-ing—both the best and the worst can come out.[14]

The outcome of such molecular transformations depends primarily on the ability of explicitly revolutionary fixtures to articulate the political and social struggles of interest. In other words, the outcome of revolt is determined not merely by a revolutionary practice, but also by a revolutionary process. This is the essential question. Without such a folding in of the distinction between theory and practice (process), all mutations of desire, all struggles for spaces of freedom, all that defines a molecular revolution, will never be able to initiate this social and economic change on a large scale.

Within this context of molecular revolution, how can we imagine revolutionary war machines of new type the are able to be grafted on both the overt and social contradictions of IWC?

Most professional activists recognize the importance of these new areas of dispute, but immediately add that in the currently moment, we must taper our expectations: 'We must first reach our goals politically before we can intervene in the everyday issues that circulate within schools, relationships, socials groups, and ecology.' Almost all left and extreme left or autonomist currents find themselves in this position. In their own ways, each of them is ready to exploit 'new social movements' which have developed since the sixties, but no one ever asks the question of how to create tools that are adapted to respond to a society of control.[15]

As soon as the traditional activist is confronted with this fuzzy world of everyday desires and practical freedoms, they are over-come by a strange deafness and selective myopia which induces a panic at the idea that a some sort of chaotically molecular and ontologically anarchistic response to IWC would contaminate the set and ordered ranks of their organizations—ranks they cling to for a sense of self.

To them, queers, crazies, free radios, feminists, ecologists and such are all a bit dodgy! In fact, when confronted with molecular agents of transformation, traditional organizations feel directed and threatened in both their militant character and their emotional investment.

Some nagging questions: How do we 'invent' new types of organizations working at the nexus of this junction that mobilize the effects of molecular revolutions towards class struggles in the Global North and struggles for emancipation in the Global South (new types that are cap-able of dissembling, case by case, the segmental transformations of IWC which render world populations as undifferentiated masses)?

How do we to fight such arrangements, which, unlike more traditional forms of organization, require creations that will not be blindsided by, or subsumed within, the technological innovations of capitalism, nor the affectively managed populations subjected to the violent experimentations of IWC at each stage of everyday life?

Nobody can de-fine today what the future forms of coordinating and organizing the molecular revolution will look like. However, it is clear that fundamentally, they involve a respect for the non-reducible autonomy and singularity of each of the components of revolutionary organization. It is clear that the level of sensitivity, consciousness, action rhythms, and theoretical justifications of more traditional party/union-based organizations do not coincide with the rupture necessary for molecular revolution. But perhaps it is desirable, even essential, that they never coincide. Through their constant co-optations and stases they will learn that their contradictions and antagonisms will not be 'solved' by retreating into a binding dialectic or organizational hierarchies that are both overbearing and oppressive.

a revolutionary, efficient war machine

What forms of organization are necessary to embody such a revolutionary ontology? Something vague, something fluid? A re-turn to the anarchic ideas of Belle Epoque? Not necessarily! From the moment an imperative to respect the features of both the singularity and heterogeneity of various segments of struggles is implemented, it becomes possible to develop, by way of delimited objectives, a new means of structuring, or blurring, questions of fluidity in the context of revolt.

As a social revolution, the molecular revolution is faced with the harsh reality that if we are to be an effective revolutionary war machine we must consider both the moment of re-volt, and, perhaps more importantly, the least static (de)institutional arrangements we plan to install the moment after the re-volt has subsided. But for such decision-making bodies to become 'tolerable,' and thus not be dismissed as mere replications of the molar power of IWC, it is essential that they be released from any 'systemocracy' at both the ideological and unconscious register. Many who have experienced traditional forms of activism to-day tend to react with hostility to any form of organization or any person who claims to preside over the administration of a meeting or the writing of a text.

Since the first and continuing concern is the junction between molar struggles and molecular investments—whether local, urban, regional, industrial, continental, or beyond—the question of the establishment of revolutionary information and decision centres must be approached from a new perspective. This requires rigorous and disciplined actions and methods radically and diagrammatically different from the programmatic systems offered by the Social Democrats and the Bolsheviks.

I will say more about this complementarity (not a mere peaceful coexistence) between:

- An analytico-political work on the social unconscious;
- New forms of struggle for freedom (such as that of a federation of groups "SOS freedoms");
- Struggles within multiple "unsecured" social categories marginalized by the new segmentarites of IWC;
- The most traditional social struggles.

The few sketches, which emerged from the sixties in the United States, Italy and France, can hardly serve as a model anymore. However, by dissecting the failure of the past we can advance the re-construction of a real revolutionary movement. In this regard, we must prepare for the unexpected, for the emergence of absurd and revolutionary character performances, for the development of subversive techniques that are still unimaginable—particularly in the fields of media studies and information technology.

Labor movements and revolutionary movements are still far from understanding the importance of this debate on such vital matters of organizational and mobilization. They would do well to accelerate their efforts to grasp the complexities of IWC—which now has the means to forge (and re-forge) new weapons to confront the upheavals that new segmentarities are able to generate. After all, IWC has no need to resort to experts on these issues—they have the systemic power to deploy new practices. Capital-ism knows how to mobilize multicentrage deployments. The complexities of administering control pose no problems to it regardless of the fact that IWC is not, and has never been, directed by one central staff or a super policy office.

As long as we remain prisoners of social antagonisms that have very little to do with the present situation, we will continue to go around in circles in our ghettos, we will remain indefinitely on the defensive, unable to appreciate the scope of new forms of resistance arising in new fields of revolt. Our conception of the world is one contaminated by the ubiquitous traces of IWC. The first of these traces is the feeling of helplessness that leads to a kind of general fatalistic anxiety.

On the one hand we have the Gulag, on the other the mouldy crumbs of capitalism. Out of this, smoky approximations of a vague socialism emerge which we can see neither the beginning of the beginning, nor our real revolutionary purpose.

Whether you are apolitical or political, on the left or on the extreme left, we seem to be locked up in a fortress—a barbed wire fence that unfolds not only over the entire surface of the planet, but also in all corners of our imagination. And yet, IWC is much more fragile than it appears. And by the nature of its development, it is destined to weaken even more. No doubt that in the future the spectres of capital-ism will be called upon once again to solve the many problems of technical, economic and social control. But the molecular revolution escapes its grasp more and more every day.

Another impetus for revolt is already gestating in our modes of sensitivity, in our relational patterns, our relationships at work, the city, the environment, culture—in brief, the molecular revolution multiplies in our social unconscious. And as IWC feels overwhelmed by these unconscious waves of molecular transformation, its power over nature, over subjectivity, over life itself nature will dissipate, and in a desperate move to recapture control, IWC will harden.

Hundreds of millions of young people already face the absurdity of this system in Latin America, Africa, Asia—they are the carriers, an inexorable wave bringing forward a different future. Neoliberals of all kinds live under the sweet illusion that things will work out by themselves in the best of all capitalist life worlds. One can reasonably surmise that the most diverse revolutionary forces are being developed in these spaces of the 'othered,' and they will continue to expand rapidly in the decades to come.

And thus it is up to each of us to determine to what extent, however small, we can work to update the policies of these revolutionary machines—for they are us and we are them—we are all theoretical, libidinal, and aesthetic machines—subjectivities imploding outward which are accelerating the crystallization of a new mode of social organization far less absurd than the insatiable monstrosity we are currently experiencing today.

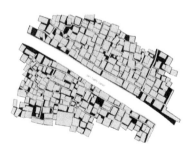

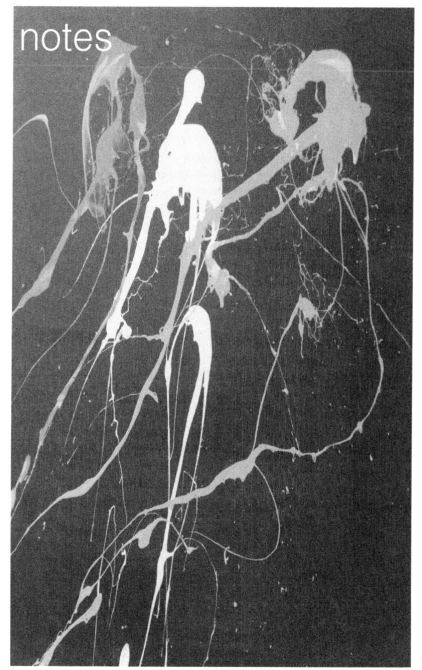

notes

endnotes

an introduction to a fractal ontology

[1] We invoke metamorphosis-machine because the term 'war-machine' has the unfortunate connotations of brutal military machinery and of uncontrollable militarist apparatuses and industrial complexes such as NATO, which operate with a machine-like rigidity and inhumanity. It is used because Deleuze and Guattari derive their theory from anthropologist Pierre Clastres' theory of the role of ritualised (often non-lethal) warfare among Amazonian indigenous groups. Instead of the metamorphosis-machine, a number of contemporary Deleuzo-Guattarian thinkers have used the term 'difference engine' or 'machine of differentiation,' and there is a lot of overlap with the idea of autonomous groups or movements in how the war-machine is theorised.

the denigration of the masses and the rise of the schizohistorian

[1] To want to specify the term 'mass' is a mistake—it is to provide meaning for that which has none. Even so, in order to get anything out of the essay one must want to specify the meaning of the term mass. The trick is to do so without giving to meaning to the masses. That is, to find its meaning through the meaning of that which it is not. While the social has particular referents—a population, a people, a class—the mass is without attribute, predicate, quality, reference. This is its definition, or its radical lack of definition. It has no sociological 'reality.' It has nothing to do with any real population, body or specific social aggregate.

[2] However, we must not intend to criticize this reification of the masses as a sloppy concept. Instead, for the schizohistorian, the masses are useful to study as an analytical endpoint. The ongoing deconstruction of class, socio-economic status, race, gender and other categories shows these 'better' tools of analysis, or better candidates for the idea of the masses have also only ever been muddled notions themselves, but notions upon which agreement has nevertheless been reached and solidified for the mysterious end of preserving a certain code of analysis—an ideological discourse that reentrenches a cultural status quo.

[3] Rather than existing in some 'real,' the media overlay on reality means we exist in statistical models that purport to measure reality but in fact are tautological, capable only of grasping what it is has already predicted and modeled. Think of the ways in which Facebook controls your Newsfeed. In a successful attempt to shape your conception of your social reality, of what your friends are talking about and what sorts of political ideas are 'important' to them, all while injecting advertisements determined through data analysis to be the least disruptive and most persuasive. Social media promises to entertain you, but this promise is synonymous with manufacturing demand—thus being entertained becomes no different from learning how to desire; pleasure is no longer desire fulfilled, but desire itself, the condition of desiring.

[4] In The hands of Donald Trump (Journal of Ethnographic Theory, 2016, Vol. 6, Issue 2), Kira Hall, Donna Goldstein, and Matthew Ingram point to the ways in which Trump's successes are due largely to his value as comedic entertainment. As late capitalism values style over content, Trump's unconventional political style, particularly his use of gesture to critique the political system and caricature his opponents, brought momentum to his campaign by creating forms of spectacle that took this characteristic to new heights.

[5] In Totality and Infinity: An Essay on Exteriority (1961) Levinas provides us with a schizohistorico-ethical grounding by articulating that alterity is not a matter of difference (in the sense of contextual, relational, determinate differences) or otherness (in the sense of an oppositional difference between the self and non-self) but rather a radical singularity that puts into question rigid social differences without appealing to a shared, monolithic identity. To understand what singularity means for Levinas, we must understand his account of transcendence, which both refers to the phenomenological tradition and diverges significantly from it. For Levinas, the transcendence of the other does not indicate an otherworldly presence, but rather a transcendence in the flesh, within finite being—only as such can transcendence open an escape from the suffocating plenitude of being. This opening of transcendence within the immanence of being makes possible a relation to the other which is not reducible to statistical comprehension or appropriation—'a relation without relation' in which the other is greeted or received without needing to become known.

[6] Instead of something distinguished from something else, what Deleuze, in Difference and Repetition (1968), calls 'difference in-itself' gives us a possibility of something which distinguishes itself– and yet that from which it distinguishes itself does not distinguish itself from it. Lightning, for example, distinguishes itself from the black sky but must also trail it behind, as though it were distinguishing itself from that which does not distinguish itself from it. It as if the ground rose to the surface, without ceasing to be ground... imagine a purely auditory universe consisting of only a single note, held at the same frequency, for all eternity, without beginning or end. This universe has no chairs, no rocks, no instruments, no particles, no zebras, no cities, etc. It consists of this single note and this single note alone without variation or change. In such a universe, this note would not differ from anything else because there would be nothing but this note. Moreover, in this universe, this note would not differ to anyone because there would be no one there to hear it. Nonetheless, I contend in such a universe, this note is a difference. It is the difference of precisely this frequency and no other. It is of no importance that it is not distinguished from anything, nor that is not observed by anyone. It is nonetheless this difference in the full positivity of its being (28).

a theory of technoanarchism

[1] From a very early age, Aaron Swartz was involved in a number of projects which constituted many of the Web architectures we interface with today. Swartz was involved in the development of the web feed format RSS and the Markdown publishing format, the organisation of the Creative Commons movement, the website framework web.py, and the social news site Reddit, where he became a partner after its merger with his company Infogam. In January of 2011 Swartz was arrested after connecting a computer to the MIT network and setting it to download academic journal articles from JSTOR.

Federal prosecutors later charged him with two counts of wire fraud and eleven violations of the Computer Fraud and Abuse Act, carrying a cumulative maximum penalty of $1 million in fines and 5 years in prison. Swartz committed suicide before his case could be brought to trial. For a further introduction to both Swartz and the seeds of this technoanarchistic ethos that he sewed, see Swartz's 'Guerrilla Open Access Manifesto,' 2008.

[2] As an ethos, anarchy replaces ideology—the good sense and common sense of the dogmatic image of thought—with meta-modelling and re-singularisation on all scales. This is an ethos of deep assemblages of collective enunciation and creation, not communication. There is no morality here—and if there is any normativity then it is only in the sense of a meta norm preferencing conditions for a full unfolding of life.

[3] For anarchists, everything is equal, but this equality is said of what is not equal, of being that differs from itself. An equality of unequals, we anarchists call it. As Deleuze (2001) says, equality lies in the ability of beings to go to the limits of their capacities, beyond their limits. This experimentation is ground, means to   endless end. It is a recognition of epistemological anarchy—the fact that what returns is difference. Thus adherents to anarchism espouse a deep opposition to authority, similarity—from this we form arguments against tyranny, property, so-called liberal democracy, conceptions of justice, and capitalism, among other things. Moreover, the anarchist objection to law is not an objection to agreement, but an objection to the imposition of rigid interpretations of what qualifies as 'right.' A frequent characteristic of anarchism is the assertion that a only law that everyone should obey is a law stating that recognition should be lived up to, for recognition is, by definition, participatory. You must recognise an agreement in order for it to apply. But for disconnected, corrupted, and/or self-interested governmental institutions to interfere in the exercise of life deprives us of our Deleuzian equality of inequality. Though often taken to mean that anarchists dislike organisation in general, this is not the case. What anarchists demand is that any institution seeking to exert influence over people should be required to prove its validity to the people it seeks to influence.

[4] As D&G (1987) point out, deterritorialisation is the movement by which something departs from a given territory—from the perspective of social change, everything hinges on the kinds of deterritorialisation present. Thus if to territorialise is to assemble information in a specific way, and to deterritorialise is to dissemble previous territorialisations, then to reterritorialise is to re-purpose deterritorialised information, not to return to previous social arrangements, but to open up new avenues of possibilities.

[5] The word epistemology is derived from the ancient Greek *epistēmē* meaning 'scientific knowledge' and logos meaning 'speech,' or 'word,' in this context denoting 'codified knowledge of.' Thus the concept is grounded on a model of 'ontology,' to designate the branch of philosophy which aims to discover the meaning of knowledge, or how we come to know. Epistemological anarchism affronts such conceptions of epistemology because it points to the unscientific nature of how we actually come to knowing the world.

[6] Dada or Dadaism is a form of artistic anarchy born out of disgust for the social, political and cultural values of modernity. It embraces elements of art, music, poetry, theatre, dance and politics. As art-factory (2015) points out, Dada was not so much a style of art like Cubism or Fauvism—it was more of a protest movement with an anti-establishment manifesto. See artfactory.org for a great introduction to Dadaism.

[7] A mode of argumentation that seeks to establish a contention by deriving an absurdity from its denial, r*eductio ad absurdum* argues that a thesis must be accepted because its rejection would be untenable—a process of argumentation grounded in the absurd. When thinking of examples of what this might look like, we point to surrealists and dadaists such as Breton (1924) and Artuad (1958), who conceptualise their works as politico-artistic performances realised in initiatives such as the conceptual art movement—a peripheral, temporal aesthetics that cultivates non-permanent art installations that expresses a politics that inherently avoids capture by its ephemeral nature, while also working to jar audiences out of their daily duties through the playful deployment of satire and irony as sites of socio-political commentary.

[8] Hayles (1987) points out, the existing society is merely the current capitalist-scientific incarnation of an ordering ontology of information—demanding the reduction of the many down to the few—a move that can be traced all the way back to the Enlightenment's stratified understanding of nature as a series of messages or codes that 'man' must decipher and order to realise his rightful domination of existence.

[9] While anarchist critiques of democracy are far too numerous to be addressed here, Marlinspike and Hart (2005) provide a good introductory critique that can be accessed free online from *The Anarchist Library.*

[10] What control produces are not so much objects, but rules (Burroughs, 1978). There is no real difference between personal affairs and politics— both represent the way control is invests itself in 'the world.' This is the concept of micropolitics—there is ultimately nothing that is not political as our economies of control are always scaled up to a broader social field. There is no Cartesian subject standing apart from the world— even our sense of personal identity is itself a product of control related to our broader social structure.

[11] By the post-representational nature of thought, we mean that genealogical thinkers such as Foucault, Deleuze, and Guattari push their critiques further than the representational notion of the individual. While many thinkers focus on the molar— individual, conscious, representational—natures of social subjection under capitalism, they fail to address the molecular—machinic, post-representational, unconscious— production of subjectivity. As Lazzarato (2014) points out, the post-representational pushes us towards the affirmative power of subjectivity because it is not only interested reconceptualising the individualising processes that equip us with a subjectivity— assigning an identity, sex, body, profession, nationality, and so on—but also how the individual is constituted as a machinic component or 'dividual' in financial, media, and state-form assemblages in a technical system in which subjectivity constitutes inputs and outputs.

[12] The practicing of privileging 'becoming' versus 'being' is grounded in the tradition of process philosophy, a tradition in which Nietzsche (1882), Deleuze (2001), and Guattari (2010) are all connected. Process philosophy is based on the premise that being is dynamic—becoming—and that the dynamic nature of being should be the primary focus of any comprehensive philosophical account of reality and our place within it. Even though we experience our world and ourselves as continuously changing, Platonic metaphysics—and essentially Western metaphysics—has long been obsessed with describing reality as an assembly of static individuals whose dynamic features are either taken to be mere appearances or as ontologically secondary and derivative. While process philosophy insists that all within and about reality is continuously going on and coming about, importantly, it does not deny that there are temporally stable and reliably recurrent aspects of reality. Rather, we take such aspects of persistence to be the regular behaviour of dynamic organizations that arise due to the continuously ongoing interaction of processes.

[13] What we refer to as the plane of consistency is a founding concept in the ontology of Deleuze and Guattari (1983, 1987)—they call it a plane of immanence. Immanence, meaning 'existing or remaining within' generally offers a relative opposition to transcendence, that which is beyond or outside—as we mentioned: Plato's *forms*, Descartes' *cogito*, and Kant's *transcendental subject*. This plane is pure immanence, an unqualified immersion or embeddedness, which denies transcendence as a real distinction—Platonic, Cartesian, or otherwise. Pure immanence is often referred to as a pure plane, an infinite field or smooth space without substantial or constitutive division. We can onceptualise the plane of immanence as plane of consistency because as a geometric plane, it is in no way bound to a mental design but rather, following from the anarchical nature of epistemology, an abstract or virtual design—a formless, univocal, self-organising process which always qualitatively differentiates from itself.

[14] These technological, biological and social processes are contingent assemblages of ubiquitous elements that include: activists, intellectuals, institutions, networks, bodies, practices, traditions, norms, behaviours, structures, signs, organisations, and informational technologies—all of which, through a loose but nonetheless coherent constellational process of territorialising past, present, and future as knowable in a specific way, flatten the amorphous multiplicities of subjectivity into static identities and objects.

[15] Following from the work of Deleuze and Guattari (1983), we take territory/terrain to be an assemblage of customs, habits, behaviours, practices defined by the functions of information. Importantly, territory is not universal. According to D&G (1987), it always has edges, ways to move through it. Yet these so-called edges cannot be thought of solely in spatialised terms—space itself cannot be conceptualised only in terms of a physical plane. For this project, what really matters are the 'edges' in terms of the meaning of signs, markers, gestures and sounds—as assemblages of a specific reading of information, these edges have specific meanings in a territory, but can be deterritorialised to take on other meanings elsewhere.

[16] The hyperlink, for example, allows all ideas to be networked—even *connected* with a proper systems theory management—it does away with a need for references or

100

sources, all *ideas* can be hyperlinked. If we recognise the products of consciousness not as products of our 'self' but as interconnected products of the sharing of information across computational networks of subjectivity, we do away with the need to reference authors—we build upon ideas themselves. This changes the relationship between producers and consumers of information—information now exists in a less fixed fashion, it can be accessed by more than one person at any time, and shared between anyone. While this was still possible for books, it was much easier to keep information hidden, and much harder to share it freely. Of course, IT still reflects the social structures of capitalism—think of the sharing economy—but hyperlinks, among other technologies I will explore—meshnets, intranet, open-source software—do open up new de/reterritorialising possibilities.

[17] Conceptualised by Frankfurt School thinkers Horkheimer and Adorno (1944), the culture industry thesis proposes that popular culture is akin to a factory producing standardised cultural goods—films, radio, magazines, etc—that are used to manipulate society into passivity. Consumption of the easy pleasures of popular culture, renders people docile and content, no matter how difficult their economic circumstances.

[18] In psychoanalytic terms, the unconscious does not include all that is not conscious, but rather what is actively repressed from conscious thought or what a person is averse to knowing consciously. Non-consciousness on the other hand is an ongoing processing of information beyond the conscious register.

[19] If we take techno-genesis seriously, then we can no longer employ traditional models of communication theory (Shannon, 1948) in which exchanges are realised between individuated subjects through emitter-receptor analogies—to go beyond an anthropomorphism we must instead speak of 'inputs and outputs.'

[20] We bring up the concept of the *meso-political*—what D&G (1987) would call thinking through a 'middle,' through the milieu (*par le milieu*)—because we fear that if we are content with the opposition between the individual and the global we are almost inexorably led to maniacal modes of differentiation where the issue is always designating paths of salvation or perdition. With the meso, it is necessary in each instance to redefine topically how the relations between the micro and the macro are assembled. In other words, it's about everything that the macro does not allow to be said, and everything that the micro does not permit to be deduced. The meso is a site of invention where the pragmatics of the question is much more alive, vivid, more difficult to forget than the micro or macro—the meso must create itself, and each time it creates, de-creates, and re-creates itself, the meso-political affirms its co-presence within a milieu.

[21] Peer-to-peer (P2P) computing or networking is a distributed technical architecture that partitions tasks or work loads between peers. Peers are equally privileged participants in the application. They are said to form a peer-to-peer network of nodes—a rhizome of inter-connections that move through the meso-level, through the middle. Peers make a portion of their resources, such as processing power, disk storage or network bandwidth, directly available to other network participants, without the need for central coordination by servers or stable hosts. In contrast to the traditional client-server

101

model in which the consumption and supply of resources is divided, peers are both suppliers and consumers of resources.

[22] Massive leaks such as the Panama Papers—which consisted of 2.6 terabytes and over 11 million records of compromised confidential information from the law firm Mossack Fonseca detailing suspected cases of money laundering and tax avoidance scheme are significant—are highly significant because they point to the larger control apparatuses operating just beneath the surfaces of popular culture, media, and democratic rhetoric. Some journalists and scholars refer to this as the 'Snowden Effect,' where direct and indirect gains in public knowledge from the cascade of events and further reporting that followed from Snowden's leaks of classified information about the surveillance state in the US and around the world have sparked public debate about the intersections of security, privacy, and anonymity that were not taking place the years prior, but should have been. For techno-anarchists, what is even more unsettling that the previous lack of debate however, is the resulting lack of political and institutional response.

'and' as a force of creative stammering

[1] Claude Levi-Strauss, *Structural Anthropology*, New York: Basic Books, 1963.

[2] Maurice Merleau-Ponty, *Signs*. Northwestern University Press, 1964.

[3] Deleuze, Gilles. *Pure Immanence: Essays on a Life*. New York: Zone Books, 2001.

an introduction to schizoanalysis

[1] Felix Guattari, *Chaosophy: Texts and Interviews 1972-1977,* Semiotext(e), 2008 (reprint edition), pgs. 67-68.

[2] Peter Sloterdijk and Hans-Jurgem Heinrichs, *Neither Sun nor Death,* Semiotext(e), 2011, pg. 147.

[3] Friedrich Engles and Karl Marx, *The Communist Manifesto*, Chapter 1.

[4] Felix Guattari, *Chaosmosis: An Ethico-Aesthetic Paradigm*, Indiana University Press, 1992, pg. 61.

[5] Gilles Deleuze and Felix Guattari, *Anti-Oedipus: Capitalism and Schizophrenia*, University of Minnesota Press, 1983. pg. 161.

[6] Gilles Deleuze and Felix Guattari, *Anti-Oedipus: Capitalism and Schizophrenia*, University of Minnesota Press, 1983. pg. 27.

[7] Gilles Deleuze and Felix Guattari, On the Line, Semiotext(e), 1983, pg. 12.

[8] Antonin Artaud, The Theatre and its Double, Grove Press, 1958.

[9] Peggy Phelan, Unmarked: The Politics of Performance, Routledge, 1993, pg. 146.

[10] Eugene W. Holland, Nomad Citizenship: Free-Market Communism and the Slow-Motion General Strike, University of Minnesota Press, 2011.

theses on the philosophy of non-history

[1] Dominic Pettman, After the Orgy: Toward a Politics of Exhaustion, New York: SUNY Press, 2002

locating the alt-right

[1] Nick Land, Fanged Noumena: Collected Writings 1987-2007, London: Urbanomic, 2011.

[2] Gilles Deleuze and Felix Guattari, A Thousand Plateaus: Capitalism and Schizophrenia, Minneapolis: University of Minnesota Press, 1987.

[3] Immanuel Kant, Critique of Pure Reason, London: Dover Philosophy Classics, 1781.

[4] Nick Land, The Thirst for Annihilation: Georges Bataille and Virulent Nihilism, London: Routledge, 1992, pg. 28.

[5] Nick Land, Fanged Noumena: Collected Writings 1987-2007, London: Urbanomic, 2011, pg.49.

[6] Jacques Lacan. Anxiety: The Seminar of Jacques Lacan. New York: Wiley, 2014.

on the necessity of destruction

[1] A more in-depth look at the concept of destruction-in-itself (as opposed to the creative destruction of Joseph Schumpeter (1942) et al.) can be found in Andrew Culp's original and fantastically desolate book Dark Deleuze (Minneapolis: University of Minnesota Press, 2016).

[2] Gilles Deleuze, Foucault, (Minneapolis: University of Minnesota Press, 1986), page: 130.

[3] Gilles Deleuze, Negotiations: 1972-1990, (NY: Columbia University Press, 1995), page: 151.

[4] While his Oedipal commitments mean we must situate Freud's work in a larger context, in Totem and Taboo (New York: W.W. Norton & Company, 1913), Freud controversially derives the illustrative figure of the 'Primal Father' from the 'Primal Horde" in Charles Darwin (1859), which Darwin defines as a great patriarchal band of brothers ruled over by an all-powerful patriarch.

[5] Hal Foster, Bad New Days: Art, Criticism, Emergency, (London: Verso Books, 2015).

[6] For more of this vitally important discussion, see Michael Hardt and Antonio Negri's Empire (Cambridge: Harvard University Press, 2000), pages: 44-45; 138-156; 190-201; 339-343

high anxiety: capitalism and schizoanalysis

[1] A system of governance introduced by French theorist Gilles Deleuze to describe the current ways in which populations are managed, a society of control is a diffuse matrix of information gathering algorithms where everything we do is being tracked, encoded, and interpreted. It does not matter if you are actually being watched—in a control society, what matters is creating the feeling you might be under surveillance at any given moment.

[2] This article will deploy a Deleuzian approach to affect (in which affects of active becoming are contrasted with those of reactive blockage), to understand transformations in the dominant regime of the control society and thus to theorize the next step for activism.

[3] To be clear, schizoanalysis does *not* romanticize asylum inmates and their often excruciating and exploitative conditions of existence—conditions which are directly fostered by the 'mental health' institutions proliferated by capitalism. As opposed to an individualized psychological 'problem,' schizoanalysis re-conceptualizes schizophrenia as a broad socio-historical system of control that results from the generalized production of psychosis and anxiety that are currently pervading capitalist society—a process that no single psychiatric patent could possibly embody.

[4] The discussion here is not fully relevant to the Global South. The specific condition of the South is that dominant capitalist social forms are layered onto earlier stages of capitalism or pre-capitalist systems, rather than displacing them entirely. The South has experienced a particular variety of affect management distinct from earlier periods: the massive forced delinking of huge swathes of the world from global capitalism, and the correspondingly massive growth of the informal sector, which now eclipses the formal sector everywhere in the 'developing world.'

[5] In 'Empire and the End of History' Rob Los Ricos makes the useful distinction between three kinds of anxiety. For the *socially included*, anxiety comes from the fear of loss of status. For *the socially marginal*, the fear of exclusion and the loss of subsistence. For the *socially autonomous and excluded*, the fear of state violence and repression. As a result, people are deemed disposable in that violent tactics can be used against anyone—even privileged subjects—without entailing any systemic illegitimacy.

[6] Capitalism is defined here as a diffuse economic and political mode of social organization that is tied together by the dominant affect of the era. In the modern era (until post-war settlement), the dominant affect was *misery*—the public secret of this

104

narrative was the misery of the working class and the exposure of this misery was carried out by revolutionaries. When misery stopped working as a control strategy, capitalism switched to *boredom*. In the mid twentieth century, the public secret was that everyone was bored. This was an effect of the Fordist system which was prevalent until the 1980s—a system based on full-time jobs for life, guaranteed welfare, mass consumerism, mass culture, and the co-optation of the labour movement which had been built to fight misery.

[7] As Reich points out, it would be a mistake to imagine that the (partial) sexual revolution of the 1960s amounts to a disruption of the underlying structures of repression—structures that cause people to feel threatened by difference and to seek to impose (not simply defend) their own way of life and to censor views which risk disclosing their irrational motives. Sexual repression does not have the centrality it once had, but sexual anxiety (i.e. sexual repression) has been diffused across the social field, displaced onto a thousand scapegoats, and the previous restriction of sexual enjoyment has been extended to enjoyment and intense commitment in general.

integrated world capitalism and molecular revolution

[1] For Guattari, the *molar* register refers to the transcendence of any models into which existence must fit—individual, representational, and conscious levels of subjugation—while the *molecular* level refers to the immanence of the process of enslavement as it unfolds within IWC—it gestures to a emancipatory diagrammatic, supra-individual, post-representational, un-conscious dimension of subjectivity that is equality as constitutive of the flows of capital.

[2] *Power formations:* sets of relationships between people, things and institutions which produce effects of domination that capture the flows of desire by territorialising events.

[3] *Socius:* the society as registered in its physical space, which is transformable along social vectors by microscopic actions that propagate in it.

[4] *Revolutionary War Machines:* temporary organizations of a formal social movement.

[5] *Layout of Desire:* we live in streams of infinitely numerous and differentiated desires that tie each being to a noticeable singularity. Every individual and collective being—including animals and plants—has a subjective consistency, with a capacity for action, an assemblage of desire driven by a libidinal economy.

[6] *Machinic:* a semiotic device that transforms the layout of desire by changing the direction of its flow—such transmissions can alter the scale and the content of desire.

[7] *Semiotics:* a semiotic device operates by directing representations, innovative actions, and transformations towards new forms of expression, as well as artistic, intellectual, and technical creativity.

105

[8] *A machinic system:* a communication system of another dimensional tempo, an assemblage of desire directed to another. This is the resumption of the cybernetic model. This machinic enslavement system creates repetitions of automation, such as those instilled by the education system.

[9] *A concatenation:* usually this concept designates a chain of causes and effects, but for Guattari, this sequence takes place in a multi-dimensional space, giving it the form and direction of the flows of desire.

[10] *A palimpsest:* a partially erased parchment which is written on again. Guattari is sensitive to traces of previous writing that interfere with any new message — it adds a degree of noise that makes it possible to draw new lines of desire for the accumulation of new signs of resistance.

[11] *A rhizome:* a way of plant growth that modulates from every angle thanks to the lack of differentiation between the stem and root. To make a rhizome is to push out in all directions, moving from one medium to another and back in a fluid movement that refuses any one-way (i.e.arboreal) formations of power.

[12] ORSEC (Organisation de la Réponse de SÉcurité Civile) plan is for widespread or long-lasting natural disasters; this does not necessarily mean many casualties, as there can be an ORSEC plan even when there are no wounded.

[13] According to Guattari, every political economy is a libidinal one — an intensity which has no equivalent in currency because it does not rid the circuits of capital of the force of libidinal investment. Intensive "exchanges" are ignorant of the constitutive negation of both political economy and natural theology since the libido invests unconditionally.

[14] For Guattari, each assertion of organized revolt also contains the ever present possibility of a counter assertion or counter-revolt. Modernity in this sense is inherently conflictual. All constructions within IWC imply a possibility of destruction and a return to a control system, especially via alternative constructions.

[15] *A society of control:* a mechanism of consumerist paranoid that results in the individualizing compulsion to manage the declining wages, precarity, unemployment, and poverty wrought by IWC in the same way one would manage a corporate balance sheet. In other words, IWC has rendered populations as guilty and responsible subjects that personally internalise all the failures of the neoliberal power bloc — especially failures externalized by the state-form and the corporation onto society. Guattari has imagined a city where, if this process continues, one would be able to leave one's apartment, one's street, one's neighborhood, thanks to one's (dividual) electronic card that raises a given barrier — but the card could just as easily be rejected on a given day or between certain hours; what counts is not the barrier but the computer that tracks each person's position — licit or illicit — and effects a universal modulation.

106

for further reading

Adams, Jason M. Occupy Time: Technoculture, Immediacy, and Resistance after Occupy Wall Street. New York: Palgrave McMillan, 2014.

Ahmed, Sara. The Cultural Politics of Emotion. London: Routledge, 2004.

Artaud, Antonin. The Theatre and its Double. New York: Grove Press, 1958.

Artfactory. "Dada: Art and Anti-Art," Artfactory, at http://www.artyfactory.org/art_appreciation/art_movements/dadaism.htm, 2015.

Avanessian, Armen and Robin Mackay. #Accelerate: The Accelerationist Reader. New York: Urbanomic, 2014.

Azar, Riad. The Occupiers. New York: Oxford University Press, 2015.

Bachelard, Gaston. The New Scientific Spirit. Beacon Press, Boston, 1985.

Bateson, Gregory. Steps to An Ecology of the Mind: A Revolutionary Approach to Man's Understanding of Himself. New York: Ballantine Books, 1972.

Baudrillard, Jean. Simulacra and Simulation. Ann Arbour: Michigan University Press, 1981.

Benjamin, Walter. Critique of Violence. London: Verso, 1927.

Benjamin, Walter. 'Theses on the Philosophy of History,' in Illuminations: Essays and Reflections. Berlin: Schocken Books, 1940.

Berardi, Franco 'Bifo.' Finally the Sky Fell to the Earth. Bologna, Italy: Seuil, 1978.

Bey, Hakim. CHAOS: The Broadsheets of Ontological Anarchism. Los Angeles: Semiotext(e), 1987.

Bey, Hakim. T.A.Z.: The Temporary Autonomous Zone, Ontological Anarchy, Poetic Terrorism. Brooklyn, NY: Autonomedia, 1991.

Boochin. Murray. Social Anarchism or Lifestyle Anarchism: An Unbridgeable Chasm. New York: AK Press, 1995.

Breton, André. Manifestoes of Surrealism, transl. Richard Seaver & Helen R, Lane. Ann Arbor, MI: Michigan University Press, 1924.

Burroughs, William S. The Limits of Control. New York: Viking, 1978.

Cage, John. Silence: Lectures and Writings on Sound. New York: Wesleyan, 1961.

Castoriadis, Cornelius. The Imaginary Institution of Society. Cambridge, Mass: MIT Press, 1997.

Chesters, Graeme, and Ian Welsh. Complexity and Social Movements: Multitudes at the Edge of Chaos. London: Routledge, 2006.

Clastres, Pierre. Archaeology of Violence. Los Angeles: Semiotext(e) / Foreign Agents, 2010.
Colson, Daniel. 1996. "Anarchist Subjectivities and Modern Subjectivity," The Anarchist Library, at https://theanarchistlibrary.org/library/daniel-colson-anarchist-subjectivities-and-modern-subjectivity.

Conio, Andrew. Occupy: A People Yet To Come. New York: Open Humanities Press, 2015.

Critical Art Ensemble. Digital Resistance: Explorations in Tactical Media. Brooklyn, NY: Autonomedia, 2001.

Culp, Andrew. Dark Deleuze. Minneapolis: University of Minnesota Press, 2016.

Debord, Guy. Report on the Construction of Situations. Paris: Situationists International, 1957.

Debord, Guy. The Society of the Spectacle. New York: Bureau of Public Secrets, 1967.

DeLanda, Manuel. War in the Age of Intelligent Machines. New York: Zone Books, 1991.

DeLanda, Manuel. A Thousand Years of Nonlinear History. New York: Zone Books, 1997.

DeLanda, Manuel. A New Philosophy of Society: Assemblage Theory and Social Complexity. New York: Bloomsbury, 2006.

Deleuze, Gilles. Difference and Repetition. New York: Columbia University Press, 1968.

Deleuze, Gilles. The Logic of Sense. New York: Columbia University Press, 1969.

Deleuze, Gilles. Foucault. Minneapolis: University of Minnesota Press, 1986.

Deleuze, Gilles. Bergsonism. New York: Zone Books, 1988.

Deleuze, Gilles. Negotiations: 1972-1990. NY: Columbia University Press, 1995.

Deleuze, Gilles. Pure Immanence: Essays on a Life. New York: Zone Books, 2001.

Deleuze, Gilles and Felix Guattari, On the Line, Los Angeles: Semiotext(e) / Foreign Agents, 1983.

Deleuze, Gilles, and Felix Guattari. Anti-Oedipus: Capitalism and Schizophrenia. Minneapolis: University of Minnesota Press, 1983.

Deleuze, Gilles, and Felix Guattari. A Thousand Plateaus: Capitalism and Schizophrenia. Minneapolis: University of Minnesota Press, 1987.

Federici, Silvia. Revolution at Point Zero: Housework, Reproduction, and Feminist Struggle. Brooklyn/Oakland: Common Notions/PM Press, 2012.

Feyerabend, Paul. Against Method. London: Verso, 1975.

Fisher, Mark. Capitalist Realism: Is there no alternative? New York: Zero Books, 2009.

Fontaine, Claire. Performance Art as Political Performance. Paris: Creative Commons, 2009.

Foster, Hal. Bad New Days: Art, Criticism, Emergency. London: Verso Books, 2015.

Foucault, Michel. The Order of Things: An Archaeology of the Human Sciences. New York, Vintage Books, 1966.
Foucault, Michel. The Archeology of Knowledge. New York: Vintage Books, 1969.

Freud, Sigmund. Totem and Taboo, New York: W.W. Norton & Company, 1913.

Galloway, Alexander R. Protocol: How Control Exists After Decentralization. Cambridge: MIT Press, 2004.

Gelderloos, Peter. The Failure of Non-Violence. New York: Left Bank Books, 2015.

Graeber, David. Revolutions in Reverse: Essays on Politics, Violence, Art, and Imagination. London New York: Minor Compositions, 2011.

Guattari, Félix. Molecular Revolution: Psychiatry and Politics. New York: Bloomsbury Academic, 1984.

Guattari, Félix. Schizoanalytic Cartographies. New York: Bloomsbury Academic, 1989.

Guattari, Félix. Chaosmosis: An Ethico-Aesthetic Paradigm. Indianapolis: Indiana University Press, 1992.

Guattari, Félix. Chaosophy: Texts and Interviews 1972—1977. Los Angeles: Semiotext(e) / Foreign Agents, 2008.

Guattari, Félix. The Machinic Unconscious: Essays in Schizoanalysis. Los Angeles: Semiotext(e) / Foreign Agents, 2010.

Hall, Kiera, Donna Meryl Goldstein and Matthew Bruce Ingram. "The hands of Donald Trump: Entertainment, gesture, spectacle," HAU: Journal of Ethnographic Theory, Vol. 6, No. 2, 2016.

Hayles, N. Katherine. Chaos Bound: Orderly Disorder in Contemporary Literature and Science, Ithaca: Cornell University Press, 1987.

Heidegger, Martin. Introduction to Metaphysics. New Haven: Yale University Press, 1953.

Heidegger, Martin. The Question Concerning Technology and Other Essays. New York: Harper's, 1977.

Iles, Anthony. Noise and Capitalism. New York: Kritika, 2012.

Jarry, Alfred. The Ubu Plays: Includes: Ubu Rex; Ubu Cuckolded; Ubu Enchained. New York: Grove Press, 1896 [1994].

Jarry, Alfred. Exploits and Opinions of Doctor Faustroll, Pataphasician: A Neo-Scientific Novel. Boston: Exact Change, 1911.

Kafka, Franz. The Metamorphosis. London: Wordsworth Classics of World Literature, 1915.

Kant, Immanuel. Critique of Pure Reason. London: Dover Philosophy Classics, 1781.

Katsiaficas, George. Subversion of Politics: European Autonomous Social Movements And The Decolonization Of Everyday Life. New York: AK Press, 2006.

Knabb, Ken. Situationist International Anthology. New York: Bureau of Public Secrets, 2006.

Krapp, Peter. Noise Channels: Glitch and Error in Digital Culture. Minneapolis: University of Minnesota Press, 2011.

Karatzogianni, Athina and Andrew Robinson. Power, Resistance and Conflict in the Contemporary World: Social Movements, Networks and Hierarchies. London: Routledge, 2013.

Land, Nick. The Thirst for Annihilation: Georges Batille and Virulent Nihilism. London: Routledge, 1992.

Land, Nick. Fanged Noumena: Collected Writings 1987-2007. London: Urbanomic, 2011.

Lacan, Jacques. Anxiety: The Seminar of Jacques Lacan. New York: Wiley, 2014.

Lazzarato, Maurizio. The Making of the Indebted Man: An Essay on the Neoliberal Condition. Los Angeles: Semiotext(e) / Intervention Series, 2012.

Lazzarato, Maurizio. Signs and Machines: Capitalism and the Production of Subjectivity. Los Angles: Semiotext(e) / Foreign Agents Series, 2014.

Levi-Strauss, Claude. Structural Anthropology. New York: Basic Books, 1963.

Levinas, Emmanuel. Totality and Infinity: An Essay on Exteriority. Duquesne, Duquesne University Press, 1969.

Lippard, Lucy R. Six Years: The Demilitarisation of the Art Object from 1966 to 1972. Los Angles: University of California Press, 1997.

Lotringer, Sylvère. Autonomia: Post-Political Politics. Los Angeles: Semiotext(e) / Interventions, 1979.

Lotringer, Sylvère. Schizo-Culture. Los Angeles: Semiotext(e) / Interventions, 2014.

Marlinspike, Moxie, and Windy Hart. "An Anarchist Critique of Democracy," The Anarchist Library, at https://theanarchistlibrary.org/library/moxie-marlinspike-and-windy-hart-audio-anarchy-radio-an-anarchist-critique-of-democracy, 2005.

Marx, Karl. 1939. Grundrisse: Introduction to a Critique of Political Economy. London: Penguin.

Marx, Karl. Capital: Volume 1: A Critique of Political Economy. New York: Penguin, 1867.

May, Timothy, C. The Crypto-Anarchist Manifesto," Anarchist Studies, at http://www.activism.net/cypherpunk/crypto-anarchy.html, 1999.

Maurice, Merleau-Ponty. Signs. Northwestern University Press, 1964.

Miller, Henry. Tropic of Cancer. New York: Grove Books, 1939.

Mitchell, W.J.T., Bernard E. Harcourt, and Michael Taussig. Occupy: Three Inquiries in Disobedience. Chicago: University of Chicago Press, 2013.

Negri, Antonio. Labor of Dionysus: A Critique of the State-Form. Minneapolis: University of Minnesota Press, 1994.

Negri, Antonio and Michael Hardt, Empire, Cambridge: Harvard University Press, 2000.

Nietzsche, Friedrich. 1878. Human, All Too Human, London: Prometheus Books.

Nietzsche, Friedrich. The Gay Science. New York: Vintage Books, 1882.

Nietzsche, Friedrich. Thus Spoke Zarathustra. Cambridge, UK: Cambridge University Press, 1883.

Noys, Benjamin. Malign Velocities: Accelerationism and Capitalism. New York: Zero Books, 2014.

Pittman Dominic. After the Orgy: Toward a Politics of Exhaustion, New York: SUNY Press, 2002

Perez, Rolando. On Anarchy & Schizoanalysis. New York: Autonomedia, 1990.

Phelan, Peggy. Unmarked: The Politics of Performance. New York: Routledge, 1996.

Plant, Sadie. The Most Radical Gesture: The Situationist International in A Postmodern Age. London: Routledge, 1992.

Portwood-Stacer, Laura. Lifestyle Politics and Radical Activism: Contemporary Anarchist Studies. New York: Bloomsbury Publishing, 2013.

Pynchon, Thomas. Bleeding Edge. New York: Penguin Press, 2013.

Reich, Wilhelm. Character Analysis. New York: Farrar, Straus and Giroux, 1933.

Scholz, Trebor. Digital Labor: The Internet as Playground and Factory. New York: Routledge, 2013.

Schneider, Nathan. Thank You, Anarchy: Notes from the Occupy Apocalypse. San Francisco: University of California Press, 2013.

Serres, Michel. The Natural Contract. Ann Arbour: Michigan University Press, 1995.

Shannon, Claude E., and Warren Weaver. The Mathematical Theory of Communication. Chicago: University of Illinois Press, 1948.

Simondon, Gilbert. Imagination and Invention 1965-1966. Paris, France: Puf Publishers, 2014.

Sloterdijk, Peter and Hans-Jurgem Heinrichs. Neither Sun nor Death. Los Angeles: Semiotext(e), 2011.

Stiegler, Bernard. Technics and Time,1: The Fault of Epimetheus (Meridian: Crossing Aesthetics). Stanford, USA: Stanford University Press, 1998.

Srnicek, Nick and Alex Williams. Inventing the Future: Postcapitalism and a World Without Work. London: Verso, 2015.

Swartz, Aaron. "Guerrilla Open Access Manifesto," Anarchist Studies, at http://archive.org/stream/GuerillaOpenAccessManifesto/Goamjuly2008_djvu.txt, 2008.

Tarrow, Sidney G. Power in Movement: Social Movements and Contention Politics. Cambridge, UK: Cambridge University Press, 2011.

Thacker, Eugene. The Exploit. Minneapolis: University of Minnesota Press, 2007.

Tilly, Charles. European Revolutions: 1492-1992. London: Wiley-Blackwell, 1996.

Vaneigem, Raoul. The Revolution Of Everyday Life. New York: Rebel Press, 1967.

Virilio, Paul. Speed and Politics: An Essay on Dromology. Los Angeles: Semiotext(e), 1977.

contributions

Printed in Great Britain
by Amazon

35199088R00071